WORSHIPING WOMEN

Re-forming God's People for Praise

HEATHER MURRAY ELKINS

Abingdon Press
Nashville

WORSHIPING WOMEN
RE-FORMING GOD'S PEOPLE FOR PRAISE

This book is printed on acid-free, recycled paper.

Library of Congress Cataloging-in-Publication Data

Elkins, Heather Murray.
    Worshiping women : re-forming God's people for praise / Heather Murray Elkins.
        p.   cm.
    Includes bibliographical references.
    ISBN 0-687-46402-1 (alk. paper)
    1. Public worship.   2. Women in Christianity.   I. Title.
BV15.E46   1994
264'.0082—dc20   94-28767
                                                                                       CIP

94 95 96 97 98 99 00 01 02 03 — 10 9 8 7 6 5 4 3 2 1

MANUFACTURED IN THE UNITED STATES OF AMERICA

WORSHIPING WOMEN

To
William Wesley Elkins
a worthy man and partner

GLOSSARY

altar-ing: to lift up the commonplace of human life to holy use.

anamnesis: the active remembering of the table fellowship of Jesus.

bricolage: "a process by which one begins with bits and pieces of traditional linguistic material, arranges some of them into a structured whole, leaves others to the side, and ends with a language ready to use" (Claude Levi-Strauss, *The Savage Mind* [Chicago: University of Chicago Press, 1966], p. 74).

catechism: the teaching of Christian life, worship, and doctrine to new Christians.

eu: "good" or "well"; **charis:** "gift" or "grace"; **eucharistein:** "to give thanks"

gender: a social-historical-political construct. "Feminine" is a gender idea. Female is a biological description. Sex-roles are complex gender patterns taught by a culture.

imago Christi: to be redeemed by Christ, and sustained by the Holy Spirit. To be an *imago Christi* woman is to be: holy and human; loved and loving of God; searching for or working in communities of faith.

imago Dei: to be created in the image and likeness of

God. To be an *imago Dei* woman is to be: created in goodness, injured by sin, transformed by grace, destined for joy in God.

liturgy: the work of the people. Worship is the proper work of the entire community of faith; a congregational participation expressing the "priesthood of all believers."

Market: "Market" is drawn from the writings of Barbara Ehrenreich and Deirdre English, *For Her Own Good: 150 Years of the Experts' Advice to Women* (New York: Anchor Books, Doubleday, 1978). "To the economic man, the inanimate things of the marketplace—money and the commodities which represent money—are alive and possessed of almost sacred significance. Conversely, things truly alive are, from a strictly 'rational' point of view, worthless except as they impinge on the Market and affect one's economic self-interest" (p. 18).

mysterion: a Greek word, "mysterion" refers to something on which silence must be kept. It is used to describe the sacramental life and language of the Christian community into which new believers are gradually incorporated.

primitive: (1) Of or belonging to the first age, period, or stage; (2) Having the quality or style of that which is early or ancient. Also, simple, rude, or rough, old-fashioned (with implication of either commendation or the reverse); (3) Original as opposed to derivative; primary as opposed to secondary (*Oxford English Dictionary*).

offertory: the communal offering of the work of human hands such as music, bread, wine, money for the work of God.

re-formation: the work of the Holy Spirit within communities seeking to be faithful to Christ. Often the process of re-formation involves unraveling and reweaving the basic structures of the community. Central to this re-formation is the work of worship.

re-member: the healing of a fragmented self or a broken community through the work of worship.

rite: the spoken words, the gestures, the performance of an act of worship.

ritual: (1) the written text of services such as baptism, marriage, burial; (2) the shared actions and interpretation of a community's life of worship. Ritual preserves the sense of a community's identity over time.

rubric: directions as to what to do in a service, such as standing for the reading of the Gospel.

theoria: "to be lifted out of one's familiar world and into the living presence of the spiritual world by a concentrated seeing" (Margaret Miles, *Image as Insight: Visual Understanding in Western Christianity and Secular Culture* [Boston: Beacon Press, 1987], p. 150).

triune: refers to God's nature, the One in Three.

sacraments: baptism and eucharist, the rites of initiation and Christian nurture. Sacraments bring the church into being, and the church sustains and reforms its sacraments.

Word of God: the creating and redeeming activity of God in relationship to humanity, revealed in Christ, proclaimed in the church by Scripture, sermon, and witness, and made alive in our hearts by the Holy Spirit.

worship: comes from the Old English word *weorthscipe:* **weorth** (worthy) and **-scipe** (-ship); to attribute worth to someone, to esteem another's being.

CONTENTS

PREFACE

The vase is heavy and holds its own on the shelves, tables, hutches, and corner cupboards of my childhood. We live in, or better, pass through, eighteen dwellings in the first twenty years of my life. Family memory, and therefore, identity, is shaped by stuff, not structures. This vase marks our particular spot in any given universe. It declares who we are, wherever we happen to be.

It arrives with my father. He has returned with it from the Korean War. Both he and the vase seem filled with a mysterious heaviness. We children are cautioned to steer clear. It is strangely weighted, made of dull brass, shaped like a Greek urn with delicate silver chrysanthemums blooming around its curve.

Its presence is felt before its story becomes part of a woman's way of knowing. It is simply there, wherever there is, as threat and as beauty. Somewhere along the way, we learn the source of its weight, the origin of its beauty. Its story is one of the few explanations he ever offers his daughters of the things he's done or seen.

War had shattered Korea, a country called "Morning Calm." Armed forces from several nations engaged in fierce, brutal struggle, yet within a people who have survived countless invasions, the cultural will to survive persists. The vase is hard evidence of their passion for life. My father holds it in his hands, turning it as he tells its story.

After a shelling stopped, village women would cautiously hunt for the artillery shell casings, discarded in the fighting. Each casing was reshaped, polished, and etched. Sometimes silver was beaten into the sides, shaped like blossoming flowers. A weapon turns into a vase. An instrument of war is re-formed into a vessel of life. The trash of war is transformed into treasure, then traded for food, medicine, and the means of life. A thing of threat becomes a thing of beauty.

Long before the biblical text of swords and plowshares was forged in our hearing, this earthen vessel taught us a truth. The strong hands of women are needed to turn weapons of death into instruments of peace. Fierce imagination, coupled with passion for beauty and compassion for life, are the primitive tools necessary for this kind of construction: hallowing the human, altar-ing the world.

This process of alteration has produced, not a book about worship, but a pre-text for worship, *Worshiping Women*. I have collected shells of doctrines to etch stories on. I have assembled a liturgical materiality of self and community from the bits and pieces of Christianity's traditions of praise and prayer. Perhaps I should attach a warning label: **Caution. This product has been altered. It is the work of a primitive mind.** This methodology has a name, *bricolage,* and a legitimate place in the study of human behavior. *Bricolage* is a process by which one begins with bits and pieces of traditional linguistic material, arranges some of them into a structured whole, leaves others to the side, and ends with a language ready to use.[1]

In *The Savage Mind*, Claude Levi-Strauss assigns this skill to a "bricoleur," a French word for janitor, or building superintendent, "someone who works with his hands and uses devious means."[2] A bricoleur "does odd jobs, drawing on a collection of assorted odds and ends available for use and kept on hand on the chance they might someday prove useful."

This "bits and pieces" approach to the sacred and historical relationships of women and worship may appear primitive, lacking in the formal manners of a theology of worship. But a primitive approach is just what the task requires, taking its meaning from direct contact, as Adrienne Rich writes in *Transcendental Etude*, "with the musing of a mind, one with her body."[3] As R. R. Marett pointed out, "The primitive encounters the divine stimulus here, there and anywhere, within the contents of an experience in which percepts play a far more important part than concepts."[4]

Percept, the sense impression of an object, makes a lasting first impression in primitive encounters with the Divine. Human perception of the holy is an intricate act of cooperation of body and mind. For many, this appears to be the natural order of a worship encounter. This is worship that is "primary" as well as "primitive." The image of a woman, seated in her kitchen, assembling her percepts of all that she encounters as holy and human, is a **primal** text of the relationship of women and worship. Worshiping women have taken their inherited bits and pieces, the threat and the beauty of the traditions of Christianity, and assembled a richly textured life of worship in the kitchen, not the formal dining room.

The formality of liturgical theology is worthy of women's attention. It is, however, secondary to the primary task of worship. *Bricolage* offers a re-formation process which meets the practical needs of assembling a worship life on its most primal level. Transforming metal shell casings into food and beauty is a tangible expression of this primal religious process.

> It uses a limited, heterogeneous repertoire of inherited bits and pieces. It makes do with whatever is at hand, with a set of tools and materials which is always finite and is also heterogeneous because what it contains bears no relation to the current project, or indeed to any particular project, but is the contingent result of all the occasions there have been to renew or enrich the stock or to maintain it with the remains of previous constructions or destructions.[5]

I come by the primitive approach, the odd jobs inclination, the devious (i.e. nonlinear) narrative honestly. I inherited it as a daughter of an oral tribe, an Appalachian family of storytellers whose identity is composed from "a limited, heterogeneous repertoire of inherited bits and pieces."[6] I learned to make do as a worshiping woman with whatever was at hand. I treasured the few texts of women who are worthy leaders of worshiping communities and those women who "altared" their commonplace of life.

Many of us are reared with an instinct to *bricolage*, formed by the limited means and meanings of women's participation in traditional worship patterns. There are few printed clues for a woman who prepares or presides at the Table. We keep each other alive by sharing a story here, a stole there. There are only precious fragments, hints of how a whole body of Christ might appear. Private disciplines of spirituality supply missing connections to formal public prayer. We search for *prae-*

texere, the pre-texts of worship. These are our realizations of the holy which can be worked into worship, using "a set of tools and materials which is always finite." [7] We set to work, transforming death into life with this bricolaged language, this bric-a-brac of praise and prayer. Sometimes we discover that such handmade artistry sets off bombshells among communities traditioned by worship orders from on high. *Bricolage* is handed on, not handed down. It can be a process of threat and beauty, but it offers an encounter with all that is human and holy.

Every text has a *prae-texere*, pre-text, a weaving together of meaning that undergirds language. It can be as elaborate as a tapestry or as simple as a thread which can be traced under, over, and through the author's design. This book's pre-text is the single word *worship*, which comes from the Old English word *weorthscipe, weorth* (worthy) and *-scipe* (-ship).[8] This literal meaning is the thematic thread which draws this work together: *worship:* to attribute worth to someone, to esteem another's being.

There are three strands of this single thread: *the worthiness of God* as known through many women's experience of the Spirit, scripture, and tradition; the *worthiness of women's forms of worship;* and the *weorthscipe of women*, the attribution of worth to women as women who are created *imago Dei.*

The Worthiness of God

"You are worthy" sing the elders, the angels, and all the living creatures in heaven and on earth.

Revelation 4:11 is the last word on holy-human relationships and that word is *worthy.* Women and men, elders and saints, join their voices in creation's chorus of praise, the cosmic act of worship. Evelyn Underhill describes this act of esteem, this *weorthscipe*, as a response of creation to Creator in her 1937 classic, *Worship*.

> Worship, in all its grades and kinds, is the response of the creature to the Eternal: nor need we limit this definition to the human sphere. There is a sense in which we may think of the whole life of the Universe, seen and unseen, conscious and unconscious, as an act of worship, glorifying its Origin, Sustainer, and End.[9]

Women's prayers are filled with the sound of blessing. There are blessings of God for rain, for relief from floods, for darkness, for light; all blessings flow from the Creator to the created and back again. We, human women made in the image of God, take our place in the all-creature choir. In ways seen and unseen, known and unknown, from the depth of our being, we esteem the One who is worthy, our Origin, Sustainer, and End. Therefore, with angels and angleworms, seraphim and salamanders, we join the unending hymn:

> You are worthy, our Lord and God,
>   to receive glory and honor and power,
> for you created all things,
>   and by your will they existed and were created.
>   (Rev. 4:11)

The Worth of Women's Forms of Worship

Two or three women are gathered: *imago Christi*.[10] The Spirit makes a quorum. Two to three thousand women are gathered: *imago Christi*. Women vest or invest their bodies and time as friends of the one named Jesus. Prophets, plumbers, and poets pray without ceasing and honor their "vocatio," call, by their daily labor and life. The stewardship of communion cups and potluck crumbs can be the chosen ministry of women in the household of faith.

We study scripture in kitchens or prisons or parks and fill in the missing names and stories. Sometimes we sing old hymns for comfort, sometimes fall silent out of discomfort, and turn to new songs for strength. Some of us open doors: Habitat for homeless, signers for the deaf, wheelchair access for the choir. Some create sanctuary in sanctuaries by the sermons they preach, or the reading programs they run. Some survive on the boundaries, speaking new structures of self and community.

A banner goes up, the sisters of Miriam dance down the aisle, but the motivation of each motion is *weorthscipe*. The final verdict of worthiness of any form of worship is not pronounced by a jury of our peers, or read from the sealed records of tradition. To truly worship, to esteem the triune being of God worthily is to trust the intercession of the Spirit within a community. "For we do not know how to pray as we ought" (Rom. 8:26). All forms of holy esteem are the only means by which *imago Christi* is revealed in the living bodies of worshiping women and men.

The *Weorthscipe* of Women

Worthy is the revealing language of a new creation.

The time has come, the chapel is filled. The trials and tribulations of the initiation rite are over. The long-awaited celebration of ordination-consecration is at hand. You and the others are led before the gathered body. You stand, facing the people of God, feeling as nearly naked as a newborn. Families, friends, and future parishioners strain for a glimpse, and then hush as the bishop turns to address them:

"We ask you, people of God, to declare your assent to the consecration or ordination of these persons. Do you trust that they are worthy, by God's grace, to be consecrated or ordained?"

The silence is less than a breath, long as death. You face the faces of those who know a little too much and those who know nothing at all. Worthy? Who is worthy . . . and the roar of a thousand voices shouts down your doubt. "Worthy! Yes, worthy! Thanks be to God."

Thanks be to God. But what of all those women of spirit who have died surrounded by silence or contempt? What of Christ's church which suffers from a discipleship of inequality? What of every daughter of God who is denied this human sound of affirmation, this roar of holy respect? **Worthy, yes, worthy! We are worthy!** you long to shout back. You vow then that every sermon will bear witness to the goodness of God who creates us female; every sacrament will reveal Christ who esteems us as companions of the Way; every prayer will draw its breath from the Spirit who labors to deliver us alive. **Worthy, yes, worthy!** is the cry of a new creation that is and was and is to come.

Diamonds Are Forever

I know the socks were new
but the dress was borrowed, just like the pool.
Everybody else got sprinkled,
but we had baptist blood on our mother's side.
So, there we stood, big girls in borrowed white like
    brides.
I kept my eyes on the buttons,
rhinestones like a river
running down banks of new breasts.

Sister went first;
water won't wash the birth order out.
I counted the times she drowned.
Once for the Father. Once for the Son. Once for the
    Holy Ghost.
He was a Trinity man.
Twice he had to call my name across the water.
I counted my diamonds, descended the steps.
One. Two. Three. Four for the four-square gospel.
What I dreaded didn't happen.
My skirt bloomed like a rose, then folded,
weighted with old mother wisdom
and washers sewn in the hem.
Tall for a new-turned woman,
the old preacher measured just shoulder-high.
Even tough as Moses,
it would take a miracle
to part the sea three times with me.

His hankie and hand covered my breath.
I clung to a button for life.
I was down to be buried in diamond-bright water,
baptized like Jesus in Jordan's deep grave.
The hard gospel sparkle strengthened its grip:
"Don't be afraid. God will lift too."

It's true.
I still have the button; came off in my hand.
I've never heard it explained,
the "how" of this part of the creed:
    "resurrection of the body."
But I need to believe;
the older I get, the younger I dream.
Learning to swim in born-again skin,
we'll wear nothing but diamonds, forever.[1]

For Inez Irons

O N E

WOMEN'S WATER RITES

Born of Water and the Spirit (John 3:5)

My father is Methodist. Our church is Methodist. Every other baptism in this small congregation involves little babies and precious little water. So why are we dressing in borrowed clothes in a borrowed church on a Sunday afternoon? My mother had been Baptist. My mother's mother still is. No question in our house that baptism is a matter of matriarchal rights. Birth water conveys baptismal water rights. Our religious identity is fully immersed in John 3:5. "Very truly, I tell you, no one can enter the kingdom of God without being born of water and Spirit." Passing through the water is a sacramental requirement for a personal relationship with this birth-giving God.

My sister and I dress in the presence of our younger sisters, our mother, and grandmother. Mother had done the borrowing; Grandma dressed the dresses up. The timing of our baptismal ritual marks it as a puberty ceremony, as well as a sacrament.

Our church is a small mission congregation, so each baptism offers the congregation an affirmation of its own life. Social approval of my sister's and my "coming of age" forms an undercurrent to the text, "You are my beloved Son. In you I am well pleased."

Grandma had done the necessary alterations, protecting us from being shamed in front of the community. Our triple immersion is inescapably incarnational. The water is warm, the primitive fear of drowning appropriate, the tenderness of the older women who dried our hair and helped us dress engenders a very human, very holy encounter. But it also signifies for me the split reality in the baptismal rights of *imago Christi* women. There is the plunge into the communal waters of tradition; we are immersed "in the name of the Father, the Son, and the Holy Ghost." There is no word or image that reveals anything other than the necessary maleness of God. The ceremonial memory of every sacrament is normatively administered by a "man of the cloth." Nevertheless, a female, corporate, body-based memory wells up within this masculinized tradition.

Incorporation

All forms of ministry emerge from the baptismal waters of the *imago Christi* community. But quantity of water does not equal quality of community, and voluntary participation does not guarantee sacramental validity. We can't simply turn on the sacramental faucet and demand holy water. The rite of baptism promises a "discipleship community of equals,"[2] which has yet to fully emerge from the waters of our corporate birth. Jew and Greek, slave and free, male and female (Gal. 3:27-28) are labels that come off in baptismal water. Distinctions based on privileged power dissolve. Distinctions based on the uniquely created *imago Dei* in each human life are not washed away.

Baptism does not dissolve the unique outlines of a woman's life into a generic shape—"Christian." A "lick and a promise" approach to human transformation is not what "putting on Christ" means. For if we "are all one," that oneness is the irreducible diversity of the triune God whose image we bear. As Marjorie Hewitt Suchocki writes,

> The notion of God as triune, therefore, has deep implications for any people naming this God as the one they serve. They will be called not to uniformity, but to many forms of diversity within community. Nor does the community of God dare to set limits to the types of diversity it can enfold.[3]

This divine image must be discernible in the daily actions of those who claim baptism. The shalom, the life, health, and peace of each is the responsibility of all. Baptism into the triune life of God marks every man, woman, child like a permanent tatoo, *imago Christi*. But this mark can only be deciphered when a baptized community boldly demonstrates the life, liberty, and love of the One who is irreducibly diverse.

Dying and Rising with Christ

In Romans 6:3-5, the burial practices of the baptized are described. We who bear the divine image, *imago Dei*, receive the imprint of *imago Christi* from the power of our baptism in Christ. We are buried with Christ by baptism into death. We are raised to walk in newness of life, dripping wet.

Jesus' baptism is the identifying "mark" of our discipleship. As Herman C. Waetjen points out in *A Reordering of Power: A Socio-Political Reading of Mark's Gospel,*[4] the original language of the Gospel states that only Jesus was baptized *into* the Jordan. All the others from Jerusalem were baptized *in* the Jordan. The Koine Greek difference between *in* and *into* is a life-and-death difference. In effect, Jesus drowned. He accepted nothingness, non-sense, death. His baptism ends his participation in the structures and values of his society. All social debts and inherited names and expectations have been canceled.[5]

In baptism, the Human One dies to the patriarchal forces which destroy the *imago Dei.* All hierarchical orders of sinful powers are washed away in the water. No question of walking on water here. Whoever accepts the baptism with which Jesus was baptized accepts the death of a socially structured identity and the resurrection of a free human being. *Imago Christi.*

Baptism is an enactment of liberation, effected by water and the Spirit. We are freed of our damaging debt to a Market mind-set, liberated from the tyranny of social location and inherited roles. In place of constricting labels, the community announces us as beloved of God, and pronounces our name.

Naming Names

It is the final hour of a pastors' retreat. We have reached a conclusion of baptismal name-calling. Pastors one-by-one are invited to sit in the center and declare the "name" they had claimed from the Word, from which they had been given the "authority" to teach and preach.

The exercise is going swimmingly until a young pastor walks to the center and sits down. We wait. Silence.

We wait. More silence. Protestant impatience with silence begins to express itself: creaking chairs, clearing throats, watching watches, and a visual counting of the bodies that are left to be named.

He finally shifts his gaze from his hands to a place over our heads. "I've looked for my name for three days. It isn't there." That cracks the silence. What does he mean, "It isn't there"? Everything necessary for our salvation is expected to be there.

"It's not that I didn't want one of those names. But they aren't strong enough. Strong enough to undo the one I have. My father gave it to me. Over and over again. My name is . . ." His gaze sinks down to his fingers. "My name is 'Not good enough.'"

There is silence, deep enough to drown in. Tears rise. We watch and listen, helpless on the shores of this grief, this dangerous confession of inadequacy. He has voluntarily stripped naked and plunged in over our heads. Modern identity is highly dependent on a self-told narrative which centers the self.[6] The gravitational power of "naming" can also create an undertow like the one in which we are caught. In a room, full of lifeguards, a pastor is drowning.

Then comes a stirring sound as a handful of women and men rise and circle the drowning man. An ancient tradition, the laying on of hands, takes place. One voice rises, then turns into two voices, then unison, male and female. "You are my beloved son. With you I am well pleased." We are deeply immersed in a renewal of baptism. What we witness is a rebirth. Such immersion is a daily need in order to pour out our newly named lives in the ministry of the baptized.

His injury has been inflicted by the masculinized mind-set of an entire culture, internalized as an inherited insult. Within a gathered community, a baptism takes place that washes all of us free of such oppressive patterns of power.

In the parking lot, I ask: "What difference will this make?" "I don't know," he replies. "Something . . ." and he touches his chest, "something in here that was broken is fixed. When I put my hand in the water, I'll remember."

Water Rites, Water Rights

The Christian memory of water rights and responsibilities has traditionally been traced to two sources, Galatians 3:27-28 and the radical equality of community described in the Gospel narratives of Jesus. There was a certain fluidity of leadership roles in the early Christian communities, but gender division quickly surfaced. The *Didascalia Apostolorum, XVI* (c. 250) formalizes the dividing of the waters of baptism for women. Women are necessary for the performance of the office of deacon, particularly for the task of anointing.

> In many other matters the office of a woman deacon is required. In the first place, when women go down into the water, those who go down into the water ought to be anointed by a deaconess with the oil of anointing; and where there is no woman at hand, and especially no deaconess, he who baptizes must of necessity anoint her who is being baptized [baptismal candidates were naked]. . . . Let a woman deacon, as we have already said, anoint the women.[7]

The social necessity of this division is clear; there is sensitivity and even a form of protection for women and men in this vulnerable act of dying and rising with Christ. Women deacons have the authority of sacramental action with women. But their right of public prayer, and the naming of God is denied. When public sacramental language is used, women are to keep silence. Only after a male authority has named God, and the sacrament is complete, does the teaching office of women deacons resume.

> But let a man pronounce over them the invocation of the divine Names in the water. And when she who is being baptized has come up from the water, let the deaconess receive her, and teach and instruct her how the seal of baptism ought to be (kept) unbroken in purity and holiness. For this cause we say that the ministry of a woman deacon is especially needful and important. For our Lord and Savior also was ministered unto by women.[8]

Dividing baptismal waters between the privilege of language ("invocation of the divine Names") and the nurture of the body (reception by the deaconess) is a split reality which still fractures our shared ministry of baptism. Yet the tide of the ministry of the baptized continues to rise. *Imago Christi* women, willingly wet behind the ears, challenge high-and-dry ecclesial structures that marginalize the power and dignity of their baptism.

One remedy for this fracture of name and body is a sacramental fusing of memory and imagination. Marjorie Procter-Smith writes of "the active remembrance of our collective past as seen through women's eyes and experienced in women's bodies. This is necessary not to fragment further the Christian community, but to restore to it that which has been missing from it."[9] Such an act of remembering requires not only collective knowing of written traditions, but a reformation of tradition through our insight, and bodily awareness of ourselves as worshiping women. Memory and imagination are required for this work of traditioning the tradition, and "only by recognizing the particularity of such remembering are reconciliation and wholeness possible."[10]

Christian baptism's erosive force is revealed in the documents of the early church. Like water working against stone, this sacrament constantly presses against hierarchical dams and divisions in communities that are to be one in Christ. The right of sacramental naming is restricted, first to male deacons and presbyters, and then to the bishop. An early church father, Tertullian (c. 200), taught that baptism was a rite that *could* be administered by laymen, but urged restricting it "on account of the Church's dignity."

> It remains for me to advise you of the rules to be observed in giving and receiving baptism. The supreme right of giving it belongs to the high priest, which is the bishop: after him, to the presbyters and deacons, yet not without commission from the bishop, on account of the Church's dignity: for when this is safe, peace is safe. Except for that, even laymen have the right: for that which is received on equal terms can be given on equal terms.[11]

Laymen meant lay*men* to Tertullian. The sacramental and social equality of baptism could neither be given nor received by women. But there is textual evidence that the effervescent baptismal water kept bubbling up through the cracks in the church's firm foundation. This evidence does not come from the canonical books, which are carefully constructed around male disciples. In the late second century, alternative narratives of women's discipleship developed into a type of Christian literature. It was an immensely popular form of literature, and dangerous to the established order because women were given central roles of discipleship in these narratives.

One such book was the *Acts of Paul*,[12] which included a section entitled "Acts of Paul and Thecla." In this narrative, Thecla is a convert who requests to be baptized by Paul. He keeps deferring her request, and she faces martyrdom unbaptized. Her self-baptism takes place in the amphitheater where other Christians have died.

> Then they threw in many beasts, while she stood and stretched out her hands and prayed. When she finished her prayer, she turned and saw a large pit filled with water and she said, "Now is the right time for me to baptize myself." And she threw herself in, saying, "In the name of Jesus Christ, I baptize myself on the last day." [13]

The transforming effect of these narratives on Christian women's identity can be measured by their critics. Tertullian attempted to control the influence that this literature had on women by citing scriptural prohibitions against women's leadership in worship. There is no mention of Galatians 3:27-28 in his interpretation of the severely limited ministry of women.

> In fact, concerning the *Acts of Paul*, wrongly attributed to him, they appeal to the example of Thecla as giving women the right to teach and to baptize. Let them know that a priest in Asia constructed this document, as if he were heaping up glory for Paul by his own effort; when he was convicted and confessed that he had done it out of love for Paul, he lost his position. For how credible will it seem that Paul gave a woman the power of teaching and baptizing, when he firmly prohibited a woman from learning? He said, "Let them be silent and question their husbands at home." (1 Cor. 14:34-35)[14]

Thecla's narrative describes a woman who chose not to keep silence. She claimed for herself the right to be named and known within the *imago Christi* community. Can contemporary Christian women, however, teach the trinitarian nature of God? Ordination rights have been granted to women in some Protestant communities, but do we have the right to name the Divine names? An ecumenical women's conference in Minneapolis provoked fierce criticism in some religious communities by naming God in an unfamiliar way.[15] But naming God is essential to the work of worship, and reforming human language is an ecumenical right and responsibility of those who bear the marks of *imago Christi.*

> But diversity need not stop with the varieties of peoples in the world—it may also address differences of theological expression. Thus the common naming of God as triune is a basis for the ecumenical nature of a church made up of diverse theological communions.[16]

The oldest form of naming the Divine names in baptism involved a threefold question, affirmation, and immersion pattern. According to Ruth Duck's water-stirring study, *Gender and the Name of God: The Trinitarian Baptismal Formula,*[17] this ancient question and affirmation pattern fully engaged the community and the believer in learning and sacramental action. This active embodiment of baptism was gradually replaced by a rite centered on a priest's recitation of the formula, "I baptize you in the name of the Father, Son, and Holy Spirit." The standardizing of this baptismal formula in the West seems directly linked to the need of the church hierarchy to establish control over diverse patterns of worship and heterodox expressions of faith.[18]

The troubled waters of baptismal controversy is an important sign of the Spirit's presence and the diversity of Christian life in postmodern Protestant churches. Some leaders want to control the boundaries of Christian life with historical formulas for worship. To recite a formula does not, however, guarantee a trinitarian depth to sacramental life. We are called to resist a superficial unity of form. To invoke "Tradition" instead of the transforming power of the Holy Spirit over our baptismal water is idolatry. If we permit only one version of the "Divine Names" of this holy and triune God, then we have named God and ourselves falsely.

Ruth Duck's suggested order of baptism restores the early church's practice of trinitarian worship framed around a tripart question-and-affirmation pattern. The mutuality of the ministry of those who are baptized into *imago Christi* is reinforced by the language and the ceremonial action of this service.

Do you believe in God, the Source, the fountain of life?

I believe.

Do you believe in Christ, the offspring of God embodied in Jesus of Nazareth and in the church?

I believe.

Do you believe in the liberating Spirit of God, the wellspring of new life?

I believe.
[Laying on of hands, chrismation, a baptismal prayer.]

N [name], Through the power of God you have been baptized into a new relationship with God and this

community. You have put on Christ.
"Whoever is in Christ is a new creation.
The old has passed away, the new has come."
You have passed through the waters of new life.
Together we join in exodus from the injustice and sin of
this world toward God's new age.[19]

Those who are baptized are uniquely created in *imago Dei*, and this is a mark of God's own irreducible diversity. This diversity is a cause for praise, not lament. Oneness in Christ is drawn from our mutual care for each other's well-being, not from enforcing formulaic obedience, or creating fear of rejection in worshiping communities. The unity of *imago Christi* is more than skin-deep, and its expression is pentecostal, many-tongued. Its life force is communicated generation to generation in the ministry of the baptized in a world which is *imago Dei*.

Thirst-Making Water

The week of fellowship, music, visuals, dance, and all the other arts is winding down. The daily services are based on the single image of a cup: the cup of blessing, the cup of Gethsemane, the cup of baptism, the cup of the new covenant. This is the morning of the cup of water, a renewal of baptism. The worshipers have been divided into households of faith, named for the communities in the book of Acts. Each household shares the leadership of house-holding.

For this service the householders are to be children between the ages of nine and eleven, the preconfirmation crowd. Each child is given a large chalice of water to hold and a sentence to say: "Remember your baptism and be thankful." It is my experience that this particular age group has a great deal of interest in being able to tell adults something, anything. This offers a rare opportunity.

The children take their places by the altar and holding the cups, hear the baptismal promises of the entire body. The ancient practice of question-and-answer takes place under their fiercely earnest eyes. The cupbearers take their places in the congregation and the invitation to renew baptismal vows is given. Young voices, "Remember your baptism, and be thankful," are heard over and under the sound of bodies flowing forward and ebbing back.

An hour after the service, a young mother asks to talk with me as I work on the paraments for the next service. "I'm afraid there was a mistake in the last service," she said. That statement is guaranteed to get a liturgist's attention.

I respond with my usual rule that if one makes a mistake in worship, it should be done with a great deal of self-assurance. I tend to cover mistakes by describing them as newly discovered practices of the ancient church.

Her doubt persists, so I ask for an explanation. It involves Robbie, her stepson, nine years old. He had been the cupbearer for their household. "Did you force him to do it?" I ask. That would have been more than a liturgical mistake.

"Oh, no, he really wanted to," is her answer, which doesn't explain the trouble. "Then?" I prod. "It's just that he's never been baptized," she responds. "Did that mess it up, you know, cancel out anybody's baptism?"

I assure her that the sacramental validity of everyone's baptism has been undisturbed by Robbie. But there is clearly more, so we take a walk beside the lake. He asked her to take the same walk after the service. They had been "mother and son" for almost two years, and it hadn't been easy. The conference was the first event for just the two of them. He had remained silent for most of their walk, inspecting the stones, tossing grass at the ducks.

When he finally got to the words, it was a question: "Can I get baptized?" He asked it, staring out at the water, avoiding her eyes. Her startled "yes" came out immediately, and then she followed with her own question. "What makes you ask, Robbie?" When I hear his answer, I am the one who is startled. "You know," he said, "saying that remembering part made me thirsty."

Made me thirsty. How many of us are thirsty for our baptisms? Where else does the thirst for righteousness come from, if not from there? A boy-child of nine had interpreted our ancient practice correctly. But the lesson isn't over.

She assures him that she would call their minister as soon as they got home and begin the arrangements. She knew he had never been baptized. His natural mother had refused any religious identity. Angry and addicted, she had died when her car wrapped itself around a tree three years before. The woman softly repeats, "It hasn't been easy." Not for Robbie, not for her.

He kept staring at the water, wanting to say something else. "Can you get baptized if you hate somebody?" What he asked was hard. What he didn't say was harder. "Who do you hate, Robbie?" He didn't turn his head, or shift his eyes from the water. "My mommy," was the answer. "My mommy. She didn't love me if she left me like that." He repeated the question. "Can you get baptized if you hate somebody?"

Where are the scholars, the ordained experts when they are needed? His question couldn't wait. "Are you worried that you said the wrong thing?" I ask. "Yes." That is her trouble. "What did you say?" I ask, hoping that the invocation of the Spirit over the water had not been in vain. "I told him, I told him the water helps with the hating."

A woman baptized by water and Spirit exercises her vocation on the edge of a lake without the assistance of experts in orthodoxy. Her interpretation would "hold water" in any sacramental gathering. Through the able teaching of his adopted mother, a midwife of spirit, a child will experience rebirth within the baptized community of water and Word. What other teachings have been lost to our common life because sacramental interpretation of our baptismal life has been limited to the few instead of the many?

Midwives of the Second Birth

As relationships between church and empire began to change in the fifth century, there was increasing theological interest in distinguishing the boundaries between salvation and damnation. Baptism became a matter of theological and political empire building. Fear of damnation, the numbing levels of infant mortality, and the doctrine of original sin as interpreted by Augustine, turned baptism into a birth rite over which only the clergy had rights. The waters of the womb were quickly followed by the waters of the font. This centering of the sacrament within the confines of the sanctuary, however, was not uniformly achieved.

Healing was women's work in the preindustrial age of Western culture. Midwives cared for women, the newborn, the sick, and the dying with healing arts and folk rituals. Midwives apparently often performed baptismal rites for the children they delivered. Evidence for this exercise of sacramental authority can be found in the repeated injunctions against the baptizing of infants by midwives.

Open rivalry and then ecclesiastical war was declared against women who were "invading" the priestly territory of male clergy, the water rites of "new birth."[20] Many midwives were also charged with violating scripture, Genesis 3:16: "I will greatly increase your pangs in childbearing; in pain you shall bring forth children." Midwives medically assisted women with birth pain and bleeding, and they offered a ministry to the *laos* (people) by the baptisms they performed. What was sacrament in the sanctuary when performed by a priest was labeled witchcraft when women exercised the rite at home. The theological struggle between the authority of the male-only priesthood and the healing profession of midwives turned violent as the church turned to the powers of the state for enforcement.

> The greatest injuries to the Faith as regards the heresy of witches are done by midwives; and this is made clearer than daylight itself by the confessions of some who were afterwards burned.[21]

What is the purpose of remembering this text? As an ordained pastor and teacher of worship, am I not committed to the authorized administration of sacraments? Baptism is not a private act, but a corporate Spirit-filled act undertaken within the community of Christ. It is essential, however, to acknowledge this history of ecclesiastical persecution directed against some women and men who exercised spiritual and social authority in their communities. Many were martyred, their torture authorized by some theologians and liturgists in order to maintain clerical power. Consigning infants to hell sounds heretical now. This medieval memory, therefore, stands guard against a modern temptation to control the worshiping life of a community by doctrine alone. The "greatest injuries to the Faith" are more often inflicted by bureaucratic blasphemies against the Spirit than by those who seek to exercise a mutuality of ministry in the community of the baptized.

The midwives in Exodus 1:15-22 who resisted the Pharaoh's "ethnic cleansing" and the medieval midwives who resisted Christendom's misogyny are part of our *imago Christi* community. This "active remembrance of our collective past as seen through women's eyes and experienced in women's bodies"[22] restores missing connections to the Christian community. We remember those whose lives are connected by water rites to our own. We exercise our water rites and responsibilities as baptized women on behalf of the past as well as the future.

When I remember the women who were midwives for my baptism, I re-member my own identity. This communal memory enables me to resist being dismembered, stripped of my identity as a woman born of water and Word. We have been formed in *imago Dei*. We bear the mark of discipleship, tattooed forever by *imago Christi*. This baptismal integrity of body, spirit, and community means we live out our ministries as midwives, men as well as women. We live and die surrounded by the community of the baptized, where women and men name the Divine Names of God, and anoint the whole people of God.

When our baptisms are re-formed by memory and imagination, we are reminded that others entered the water before us. We are never alone. I can lay claim to other sisters, other brothers known and unknown, living and dead, who have passed through the waters. To be *imago Christi* women means we choose to be sisters to ourselves and others. We choose to be who we are, and who we are means we are *for* each other. We make a "sister choice," choosing to sister ourselves and be kin to other women.[23]

> Choosing to be a woman or a man means not just settling for what we are but accepting ourselves, in our own body, with our own abilities, race, sexuality, family, class, and culture, as a gift of God. Women of all colors have ultimately to make this choice as they recognize that who they are as a woman is not given but constructed out of their own situations and response.[24]

Christian Vocation

Baptism is a sacrament of Christian vocation. The anointing of Jesus by the unknown woman found in Mark's Gospel (Mark 14:3-9) is an exercise of baptismal vocation. She knows who he is, what he will do, and prepares him for his baptism. To recognize the anointed ones of God in a world where oil and water don't mix is part of our baptismal call. What Tertullian wrote holds true, "for that which is received on equal terms can be given on equal terms . . ." Discernment of Spirit and nurture of community is the vocation of all baptized women and men. Daily interpretation of this sacrament *is* an ordained responsibility for all who have been baptized.

The Spirit moves over the water, sometimes stirring, sometimes troubling, always offering challenge and choice. Some feminist theologians favor immersion and adult baptism for women because of this sacrament's "equal rights amendment" and its physical and spiritual power.[25] Baptism, similar to Eucharist, is a sacrament filled with female symbols. One form of holy-human water-sharing takes place when women who have given birth compare stories. But our relationship to water and Spirit cannot be limited to birth narratives. Perhaps a warning sign should be posted by the font: "This rite is not a parental right."

> The symbolism of the baptismal font as womb in which new Christians are conceived and from which they emerge as children of God is once again problematic for many women. While it is a relief to have a symbol with which most women can identify, for others, it is yet another assertion that the special role—indeed, the only worthwhile role—of women is to bear children.[26]

To be baptized *imago Christi* is to become fully human, and claim the changes of life and death and life beyond death. We carry all our social and biological roles into the water, but when we rise, we rise as free human beings, bearing the image of the triune God. This powerful re-formation of identity has its origin in this means of grace, yet we daily reclaim the name which the living God has given us, "Beloved." Our life-long work is the work of John. We must identify the signs of the Messiah, where and whenever Christ appears. Our baptismal conversion enables us to be about this work of worship, praising God, not paying homage to principalities, or subverting the freedom of the gospel through gender.

> When Christians intentionally or unintentionally pay homage to the powers of this world, they subvert the primary goal of worship—to thank and praise God. To

exalt masculine gender expectations and to support male privilege through association with the God of Jesus Christ is to subvert true praise and thanksgiving.[27]

Conversion as Purification

Thirst quenching is a challenge for individuals and communities at the close of this century. Some suffer an immense thirst for "authentic" experience. Some are saturated with toxic levels of violence and inhumanity. Where can we find living water?

In John 4:5-30, a Samaritan woman asks Jesus the same question. This encounter is a wellspring of images of conversion. Aruna Gnanadason, director of the World Council of Churches Subunit on Women in Church and Society, reflects on this scriptural account through the experience of Indian women's water jars. In India, water jars are polished examples of the human need for survival. The polishing could be seen as domestic slavery, or a creative expression of a woman's relationship to nature. The water pots are also used politically when Indian women stage public demonstrations, demanding clean water from government officials. By linking these experiences of ordinary women to the scripture, the story of the woman at the well recovers its converting power.

> The Samaritan woman's first impulse when she receives the message of freedom is to leave her water jar behind (v. 28) and go into the town to share the good news that she has heard. . . . Her leaving of the water pot behind is proof of her determination to leave behind her life of oppression and sinfulness, so as to internalize the liberating power of the living water.[28]

Holy-human meaning bubbles up from the sacrament of baptism like an artesian spring. Dying and rising with Christ, new birth, a sign of the kin-dom of God, naming, anointing with the Spirit, conversion, and purification are just some of the dimensions of this sign-act.

Purification is one that requires reinterpretation. Our consciousness of injustice leaves a bitter taste in our sacramental water, raising a question of symbol pollution. Water has served as a natural symbol of holiness in every religion. It is the most ancient and universal of religious symbols. In Genesis 1:1-2, darkness and waters are the matrix from which the Spirit draws light and life. "The earth was a formless void, and darkness covered the face of the deep, while a wind from God swept over the face of the waters." What can't be masked by modern convenience is the troubling of these creative waters of the world.

We in North America now know that we are drinking deadly lead, pesticides, unpronounceable toxins, and lively, nasty microbes straight out of the tap. What happens when a natural symbol, water, source of sacramental identity, turns toxic? Can we convert this natural symbol back to its source through our narratives of baptism? If we could follow the stream from font or pool back to its place of origin through an act of liturgy, would it "altar" our economic and social choices?

Many congregations have reclaimed a form of thanksgiving over baptismal water that includes a recitation of the history of water and the Spirit. This is not a matter of liturgical innovation, but purification. The purification or sanctification of baptismal water, requires conversion to the mission of defending creation. Work and worship are the two hands of prayer that emerge from the sacramental waters of baptism. Purification in this sense means getting our hands dirty as we assist in God's act of sanctifying the waters of creation.[29]

Women are the water-bearers for most of the world's communities and often walk miles for precious drops of water. Long before the water is poured into a font or bowl and blessed, it has been cupped by a woman's hands, carried on a woman's head, distilled from her sweat.

Such responsibility for gathering of water is rarely a question of women's rights, or rites. So how can this painful reality become, in Augustine's words, "a sign of the grace of God and a form of invisible grace, so that it bears its image and exists as its cause"? Can this sacrament signify and sanctify a human community of equality and grace? A baptismal liturgy should invoke the sound of mighty waters and the rumble of holy righteousness.

Sign of the Kin-dom of God

Located in Montgomery, Alabama, is a memorial monument where hundreds of baptisms take place every day. It was designed by Maya Lin, architect of the Vietnam Memorial, for the Southern Poverty Law Center. It is built of black granite, etched with forty names and a paraphrase from Amos over which water cascades then stills: "until justice rolls down like waters and righteousness like a mighty stream."

The last name recorded is the source of the prophetic paraphrase—Martin Luther King, Jr.—and the quote was the wellspring for the memorial. Maya Lin described her process of "symbolizing" to journalist William Zinsser:

The minute I hit that quote I knew that the whole piece had to be about water. I learned that King had used the phrase not only in his famous "I have a dream" speech at the Washington civil rights march in 1963 but at the start of the bus boycott in Montgomery eight years earlier, so it had been a rallying cry for the entire movement. Suddenly the whole form took shape, and half an hour later I was in a restaurant in Montgomery with the people from the Center, sketching it on a paper napkin. I realized that I wanted to create a time line: a chronological listing of the movement's major events and its individual deaths, which together would show how people's lives influenced history. . . . Unlike the Vietnam Memorial, which covers a specific period of time that's over, I wanted the Civil Rights Memorial to deal not only with the past but with the future—with how far we still have to go in a continuing struggle.[30]

The location of this woman's memorial marked another woman's witness to the struggle. Montgomery is where Rosa Parks refused to give up her seat and set in motion the thirteen-month Montgomery bus boycott. Her name we remember; Maya's sculpture remembers for us the names we have forgotten: Emmett Till, a fourteen-year-old Mississippi boy killed for simply speaking to a white woman; Addie Mae Collins, Denise McNair, Carole Robertson, Cynthia Wesley, killed in the bombing of the 16th Street Baptist Church in Birmingham, 1963; Viola Gregg Liuzzo, a civil rights worker and mother from Detroit shot by the Klan for driving freedom marchers; Jimmie Lee Jackson, who died trying to protect his mother and his grandmother from the violence of Alabama state troopers.[31]

The names are incised on a round tabletop, almost twelve feet in diameter, but set low enough for a child to reach. Water rises from the center of the table and covers the names. It is a tangible expression of our sacramental life: table and font together.

The water is as slow as I could get it. It remains very still until you touch it. Your hand causes ripples, which transform and alter the piece, just as reading the words completes the piece.[32]

There is a further altar-ation Maya had not expected at the dedication ceremony, yet happens repeatedly: tears. "I was surprised and moved when people started to cry. Emmett Till's mother was touching his name beneath the water and crying, and I realized her tears were becoming part of the memorial."[33]

This civil rights "font" mirrors back the *imago Christi* to Christian communities. Set at the entrance to a Law Center dedicated to seeking justice and resisting evil, it reforms the tradition of the baptismal font of Christianity. Our baptism belongs at the entrance of our corporate life in Christ, and its mighty stream of righteousness can be stirred by our tears.

We do not need the kind of forcible public baptism that took place under the colonization of Christendom. But here is the concrete expression of a woman's baptismal imagination, her authority as symbol maker. Here is the signifying and the sanctifying of a sacrament that creates a public witness of baptism. We touch the names in the water and are strengthened "to deal not only with the past but also with the future— with how far we still have to go in a continuing struggle."[34]

To invoke the Spirit through the stories of spirited women is a necessary part of "altar-ing" our reality as women. How do we avoid drowning in sacramental generalities or political strategies? Time and time again, I return to a story of one real flesh-and-bone woman.

Gift of the Spirit

The rain began early in the November afternoon. Fall rains are expected in West Virginia, often needed for life in the coming spring. But a rain that comes too heavy, too hard against the hard-edged hills, is a killing rain. The rains come down and the floods come up, come up fast, almost overnight.

Lives are lost in the undertow of rivers and creeks gone wild. Hundreds of homes, businesses, and churches are destroyed. Communities trying to tread water economically watch the future wash away. No human effort can turn the tide.

By June (Annual Conference time for United Methodists) the entire state had received an outpouring of compassion and action. Help and helpers had come from neighbors and strangers a continent away. We needed worship forms that could channel the grief and the celebration. "A Service for the Renewal of Baptism" was chosen. Water had destroyed. Water might heal. The passage from Romans 6:3-5, "We have been buried with him by baptism into death," needed little verbal interpretation. Those who gathered understood on a gut level what it meant to be buried in the waters.

The gathering of those who had been baptized, laity and clergy, was also a gathering of waters. One by one, the waters of West Virginia and Garrett County, Maryland, were named. At each name, a person would rise and come forward carrying a mason jar filled with the "killing" water. Others stood as their river, pond, or creek was named. Their lives had been "baptized" by the water now being gathered in a large crystal basin. The bishop stretched his arms over the waters and invoked the Spirit, which had led the people of almost heaven through the flood.

Old gospel songs like "Showers of Blessing" shimmered with the unshed tears. The altar was adorned with a quilt pieced together from some of the shirts, skirts, coats, and blankets sent for flood relief. The central image in the quilt design was a pink rose. When the time of witness came, the story of the rose was told. A clergywoman had managed to reach the home of one of her widows as the waters receded. Her possessions of a lifetime were buried under mud and crushed ceilings. The two women lamented together, then walked outside holding hands. Devastation. They rounded a sinking corner of the house and encountered a miracle. One delicate pink rose in full bloom. One pink rose in the midst of muddy destruction. The sight took their breath away and restored hope the same way. The story of two women holding hands in front of a rose "altared" the grief of hundreds who had passed through the waters of death. Together we rose to a new hope in Christ. K. Almond, one designer of the service, writes:

> Attending to human experience, especially the experience of women who seem often to weave together the threads of their families and communities, is vital if hope is to be life-giving and holy, rather than a seductively simple substitute. Hope is the ongoing "project" of Christian worship.[35]

These witnesses to the work of Word and Spirit recounted their deliverance, their "project" of hope in the service of worship. Time was made holy by the telling of these very human stories. The last one to rise was in her eighties, a member of one of the black United Methodist congregations. She didn't need the mike, her voice filled the packed chapel.

She and her older sister hadn't minded the rain, she

said. The creek beside their home hadn't overflowed its banks in more than a hundred years. They didn't worry as night fell and the waters rose. When the raging water reached their porch, there was no way for help to arrive.

She sent her sister up to bed. She was younger and "always a bit bossy." She waded through the water, which poured into the first floor, to retrieve dry coats and their brand-new vacuum. Once upstairs, she put the vacuum in the bathtub to keep it high and dry. She closed the curtains against the sound of the flood, then spread the coats on their bed. She got into the high old bed where she and her sister had been born. Over the sounds of destruction and in the face of death, they held hands, said their prayers, and laid down to sleep.

The next thing she heard was a terrible howling. The sound shattered their sleep. The room was cold, dark, and unfamiliar. For a moment, she thought she had died and gone to hell, then gradually, her senses sharpened. She and her sister were still in their house, in their bed, dry as toast. She got up and made her way to the window, the source of the unnerving howling. She drew back the curtain. Two things were instantly clear: the water was going down, and the howling came from an ordinary dog, very wet and unhappily perched on their second floor air conditioner.

Laughter burst through dammed up tears with her revelation. We then lapsed into silence as she thanked God, who had, once again, carried her safely over Jordan. In the middle of her prayer she started to sing. I have heard "Amazing Grace" many styles, many places. This is the sound I'll always remember: an old woman's voice, filled with wisdom and Spirit, moving on the face of the waters.

Stirring Women

We are stirred by a sense
   as common as spoons.
   Amen.

We are capable
   of cupping God.
   So be it.

We believe in the destiny of dining.
We ladle grace like gravy
   over the bread of life.

In a hard-to-handle time
   we are good at getting to the bottom,
   gripped in Necessity's hand.

We invent perpetual motion
   from a rounded shape
   and a hungry sound.

Few if any
   are born to the taste of silver.
Most acquire stainless steel.

We inspect tear spots,
   polish teaspoons
   using a trace of acid.

Let others sharpen their wits,
   pare away distinctions,
   separate the jointedness of time.

We are spoonfed, start to finish.
Stir, lift, and blend mercy,
   served warm.

Let us be godly as spoons.
   So be it.
   Amen.[1]

T W O

FEASTING IN A FASTING AGE

Remember to Say Grace

On the south wall of an unstarred diner on the Pennsylvania interstate hangs an image of holy dining, an icon of a woman feasting in an age of fasts. I had stopped for safety's sake, preferring to nod off while drinking, not driving. I unwrap a sandwich of indestructible parts. I focus on the picture above my booth to avoid the nosy eyes of the all-male late-night diners. Apathy. Interest. Epiphany. It takes three blinks. An old woman, a young boy, a diner crowd of cynics. Her head is bowed. His head is bowed. She is saying grace. A Rockwellian vision of *eucharistia* of a once-civilized religion.

What embarrasses and convicts me in a flashpoint is the gut-level power of a woman saying grace in a graceless place. She does not ask permission or participation. She "altars" the scene by refusing to distinguish between a private and a public sphere. What she does at her kitchen table, she does in the world. Her head is bowed, her hands folded, yet there is social power in this seemingly passive gesture. She is old, as socially vulnerable as the young boy who prays with her. Yet her dignity and refusal of social compromise, her struggle for survival, her sense of her-self in communion with God-self was arresting.

Does the coffee-laced trucker see what I see? Does the fast- and faster-order cook know there is an icon on the south wall? For me, this image is insight.[2] I am "lifted out of one's familiar world and into the living presence of the spiritual world" by a concentrated seeing.[3] This seeing or *theoria* is a necessary discipline for discerning women's sacramental life. Our social and religious environment, however, has restricted visions of holy dining to "The Last Supper" and relegated women to the tip on the table. This imaged act of an old woman's *eucharistia* is not an exercise in nostalgia but a revelation of women's sacramental life. It extends its prophetic reach to every table laid in Christ's name.

To remember and *to say grace*, memorial and thanksgiving, are two of the doctrinal dimensions of the sacrament of the Eucharist connected to scripture and experientially linked to the social location of women.[4] Complex theological explanations of the form and function of *anamnesis* have been written and forgotten. Ink and blood have been spilled over the nature of Christ's bread-body connection. *Eucharistein*, the making of thanks, the breaking of bread might become an agreed-upon table manner for our separate communions. But we will need to alter our tables. The shape of table fellowship that helps us remember to give thanks is round.

> The round table has become a symbol of hospitality and a metaphor for gathering for sharing and dialogue. It speaks concretely of our experiences in coming together and connecting at home, at work, and at worship; it also points to the reality that often persons are excluded from the tables of life, through denial of shared food and resources and through denial of shared naming and decision making for their community, nation, or world.[5]

52

This round table provides a prophetic edge which enables the church to "remember into the future." This "futuring" is also an *anamnesis* of the historic table fellowship of Jesus found in Luke's account of the Last Supper (Luke 22:19) and Paul's descriptive revelation (1 Cor. 11:23-24). The earliest table prayers from the *Didache* were filled with the grammar of Jewish blessings and the exultation of a community gathered in *eucharistein* at the table of Jesus, the *child* of God.

> Thou, Lord almighty, didst create all things for thy Name's sake, and didst give food and drink to human creatures for their enjoyment, that they might give thanks to thee, but us hast thou blessed with spiritual food and drink and eternal light through thy child. Above all we give thee thanks that thou art mighty. To thee be glory for ever.

Remembering, giving thanks are profoundly human responses which sanctify a human necessity, eating. The sound of a round table grace can be as ornate as *The Cherubic Hymn* of the Divine Liturgy or as simple as a kiss. The most sacred gesture in Christianity is the offering of bread-host-body to the believer. Protestant worship focuses more on ritual speaking than eating, but this oral dimension of the "Word made flesh" makes Christianity distinctive. As Ronald L. Grimes points out in *Beginnings in Ritual Studies*, "The Christian bodily style is fundamentally oriented around consuming and communication."[6]

Women are almost universally responsible for feeding and the teaching of language. Christianity's primary forms of worship are communion and communication, but the authority for these forms of eating and speaking has been restricted to men. More women are now invoking memory and grace with public sacramental power. The number of women graduating with Master of Divinity degrees rose 224 percent between 1977 and 1987.[7] Many mainline congregations, such as the Episcopal Church, are experiencing this surge in female communion and communication.

> But in a sacramental church, the most earthshaking change was the entry of women into the ordained clerical role and its central act of worship, the celebration of the eucharist. What does it mean for women to receive the bread and wine from the hand of a woman for the first time? How do laywomen now think about leadership? Whom do they see as capable of being leaders, within their congregation? What effect does a changed image of religious authority have on other relationships and symbols?[8]

These are critical questions for the re-formation of worship for God's people. A woman's right to commune and communicate *anamnesis* and *eucharistia* cannot be disconnected from the challenge of establishing the sacramental fellowship of a round table. All our *painful* "isms" are formidable barbed-wire fences we erect around this table. Merely trying to name the barriers separating Words of Institution and the language of a soup kitchen is more than a mouthful. Reformation is needed, but is it possible to re-form a culture that is revolutionizing at a bewildering speed?

Give Us This Day Our Daily Bread

All forms of family eating have rapidly changed, losing their distinctive style, their force of habit. In this cultural turning of the table, however, a Market icon is created.[9] A Rockwellian family fantasy burns an after-image on our imagination. Surveys of the patterns of family dining and praying indicate we "remember" eating together and saying grace.[10] We remember; we are not "doing this in memory." Is our cultural memory of holy dining based on real experience or virtual reality? Can it be realized in a corporate manner that is liberating, not addicting?

Our private life of love and food shapes or suppresses our corporate experience of sacrament. The way to anyone's heart is, indeed, through the stomach. The sense of taste and the sense of self-esteem and self-control are intimately joined in our earliest experiences of food. But what happens to the self-esteem of the one who must feed herself and others while on a cultural starvation diet with limited social and economic choice? Daily bread, and little more, is the daily fare of many women in rural and urban areas. The decade of international, ecumenical study of the social location, or more accurately of the dis-location of women, puts it bluntly: women are earning less, working more, and getting poorer.[11] In our time, one out of five families is headed by a woman, and one-third of those families live below the poverty line. The "average" woman will spend seventeen years caring for children and eighteen years caring for older family members.[12] Women's economic insecurity makes the Lord's Prayer prophetic, "Give us this day our *daily* bread."

One vision of North American cuisine is displayed in a side window of a New York City art store. It is a dollhouse, delicately accurate in its miniature reality of a family's Thanksgiving. The mother of the house is at the sink, wearing a red-checkered apron. The father is standing at the head of the table, which is graced by a tiny turkey, a bowl of mashed potatoes the size of a dime, and a thumbnail loaf of bread. The offspring are arranged in descending order, large to little, bodies turned toward the turkey, in anticipation of the feast. It would be a scene straight out of Rockwell's "Freedom from Want" except for the fact this is a family of roaches. Real roaches. Dried and dressed and arranged into artwork with an attitude. The price tag prevents it from being prophetic on the part of the artist. But the image is insight, *theoria:* in one of the world's great cities, only the roaches have reason to give thanks.

Thanks-giving is an act of *doing* which is required for *remembering.* In a culture where bread is a matter of irrelevance to survival, holiness still flavors the prayers. We do not live by bread alone. But the prayers of the poor hold the power of need *and* remembrance. As Janet Morley writes in her collections of prayers, *Bread of Tomorrow:*

> Most of us find the Lord's Prayer familiar and comforting, not unsettling or full of painful longing. Not actually hungry for bread, most of us pray for spiritual stamina day by day. . . . Many Christians in the poorest parts of our world pray quite differently. They pray for real food, but they are also hungry for justice.[13]

Breaking bread and sharing the means of earning that bread are not a tabled agenda in the re-formation of worship. If we remember to say grace and forget old Mother Hubbard's bare cupboards, we suffer amnesia.[14] This amnesia blocks true *anamnesis,* the active re-membering of the table fellowship of Jesus. Simply being fed does not guarantee that grace will be meant or said. What enables us to bless the hand that feeds us?

My own catechesis began with feeding and being fed and learning to say "Thank you" at my mother's mother's table. I moved from spoon to fork in a matrixed family setting. My mother did not cook, she "worked outside the home" for the basic necessities of food and shelter. Grandma inhabited the private sphere of woman, food, and grace.

Bread was a weekly fragrance; store-bought was a sign of sloth. If I reconstruct the reality of her table, I must admit that she was a plain cook, heavy on the starch. Fried mush and potatoes were the staples that poverty provided us. She and her "Mister" had owned a grocery store during the Depression. They kept dozens of families from starvation with credit, which was never repaid. The loss of the store returned Grandma to the kitchen.

Woman. Food. Grace. It was a century-long relationship. She peeled apples for pies when she turned 91; chopped carrots by touch when her eyes gave out at 100. By 104, her role at my sister's kitchen table was a stirring one. At 106, she finally experienced the difficult change of life: going from feeding to being fed. But her gratitude for daily bread was also her aptitude for grace.

I have framed her final lesson. It hangs on my memory's wall. My older sister's kitchen is filled with the noisy smell of dinner. The cousins are not kissing, but thumping each other on the arms as young males do. Sandy has inherited Grandma and her apron strings, so we, younger sisters, do as we are bid. My assigned chore: feed Grandma. It is the safest task in an intergenerational, intra-sibling negotiation called Thanksgiving.

In a kitchen with too many sisters who know one another too well in too few ways, we skirt the boiling points. When things heat up, we sing songs, our common heirloom from our mother. "Over the river and through the woods, to grandmother's house we go."

Turkey is now beyond Grandma's ability or interest. Long after other tastes have departed, the sense of bitter and sweet remains, so she is having dessert. I spoon-feed her ice cream, attention elsewhere, until she stops the spoon with her hand. She traces the spoon to my fingers, kisses my hand, then happily retraces her way to the spoon. A primal gesture of gratitude for being fed. A simple eucharistic gesture. To kiss the hand that feeds you.

Remembering to say grace, to make thanks requires eucharistic living in its most elemental form. This learning to remember goes deep into our corporate body when liturgy and life share in the common goods that a Eucharist offers. We are, start to finish, spoon-fed by grace.

Those who have experienced this primary form of female-food connection as a reason for "eucharistia" draw on this natural symbol in the sacrament of the Table in ways that liberate it.[15] It is not simply a matter of having a woman preside at a communion table. Ordination is a precious right of *imago Christi* women, but it does not "solve" the problem of the unjust relationships in what should be a "household of freedom."[16]

Just as the process of women and ordination is not, in and of itself, humane, neither is the gendered relationship of women and food in and of itself holy. Nevertheless, the remembering, *anamnesis*, is a re-membering, a re-collection of our earliest relationships of women and food. This re-membering, re-collection may enable us to resist the cultural forces of amnesia, which strip our lives of their sacramental potential.

Because There Is One Cup

One of our oldest texts of table grace comes from *Apostolic Tradition*, a work attributed to Hippolytus (c. 170–c. 236), presbyter and martyr of the church in

Rome. For some communities in his time, Hippolytus was a worthy challenger for the chair of Rome; to other interpreters, he was a schismatic, bordering on heresy. His eucharistic service, however, not only survived the terrors of history, but thrives. It is the basis for many of the re-formations of this sacrament in this century, even though it suffered through poor translations and exists only as a reconstruction.[17]

I remember the jolt of my first reading of the Hippolytus service in Bard Thompson's classic, *Liturgies of the Western Church*.[18] A well-kept secret emerges in its ancient rubrics. How many cups were on this table? Three, not one. What were the other two and where did they go?

The first cup offered to the newly baptized was a cup of water. The inner washing of the spirit was as necessary as the water through which the body passed from death to life. Those who hungered and thirsted for righteousness were given water to drink for the "inner washing" of the spirit. The third cup is now our one and only, the cup of the new covenant. The chalice of wine, the fruit of the vine is the familiar curve which we recognize. Missing from our memory and our present identity is the second cup, a cup of milk and honey. This missing cup was given to "the children of God for the healing of the bitterness of the human heart with the sweetness of His word." So reads one of the earliest communion texts of Christianity, revealing a God who feeds the young, teaches them to speak, and yearns for their healing.

Why did we leave this cup off the table? What permitted the forgetting of this very female cup of milk and honey? What might be "altared" if we remembered this cup? Would the institutional structures we have constructed from the institution narrative ("Do this in memory of me") be re-formed if we returned this cup to the table? A cup of milk and honey, given for the healing of the bitterness of the human heart with the sweetness of God's Word.

The Proper Feeding of Children

In the practice of the early church, new Christians followed a ritual patterned on images of the nurture of the young. Christian initiation rites separated believers from the "adult" knowledge of the world, restored them to the state of little children, fed them, and taught them a new language, the language of prayer.

New Birth. Bread. Water. Milk and honey. Wine. First words: "Teach us to pray." This connection of sacraments was seen as a "natural" progression for every one "born of a woman." The early believers were lifted from the new birth waters, then blessed, breathed upon, and fed. But the "naturalness" of this connection has been broken in many traditions by the forcible separation between new birth and feeding.

Many Protestant churches have held the young at a distance from the table until they can formally express their hunger. Confirmation was modeled on public education, and the mastery of conceptual language. Children were to remain silent, absent from the table fellowship until they could discuss doctrines. Sacramental eating remains largely an adult activity, clearly separated from the daily feeding of children.

Nevertheless something is shifting in our theological table manners. A retired pastor voices the surprising anger he feels when he visits a colleague's communion service. It is a World Communion service and the adults are invited to come forward to receive the elements. After they return to their pews, the pastor invites the children to join him beside the table. He points to the empty cups and crumbs, explaining: "This is a special meal for the friends of Jesus. Someday you will be old enough to eat here and do the things that Jesus wants his friends to do."

What strikes me is how the visiting pastor voices his criticism: "What mother would make her children watch her eat and tell them that someday they would be old enough to be fed?" His perception of maternalness of this sacrament turns the tables on a mind-over-body model of Christian education. The openness of the table to children represents a shift in our Protestant *oral* tradition: first communicate, then commune. To commune, and through that communion, communicate, restores the natural order of holy, human development.

There are female images in, under, and through this sacrament, below the surface of language. Woman = food + child = life. But there are recognizable troubles in this equation. To "be born of a woman" is one defining reality of being human. The early church affirmed Jesus' humanity in those terms in the Apostles' Creed. To be a mother, however, is not the defining reality of being a woman. The Protestant church in particular, needs to be on guard against its own inclination to idolize the cultural images of family.[19]

But something essential in holy-human relationships is suppressed when our language of praise and prayer is deprived of female images or demurely limited to the "Bride of Christ." Female embodiment still carries a culturally induced virus: shame. Contemporary prayers that frame language out of female experience run the risk of being labeled heretical or pornographic, anything but holy. A redeeming vision of these *imago Dei* images may have to come from the past, not the present.

Body as Holy Food

The scene is drawn in miniature, a richly detailed context wrapped around a text. A doctrine known as Double Intercession illuminates the corner of a page in a mid-fifteenth-century Book of Hours of Turin-Milan.[20] Enthroned in gold and glory the Father sits, regal and stern, judge of all nations and nature. Mother and Son kneel beside the throne, each offering to the Father a form of embodied love for the sake of humanity. The Son cups the blood, which pours through the wound near his heart. The Mother cups her breast, offering to God and the memory of the viewer, the milk of human kindness and faith. This is an earthly banquet for the eyes of a believer, a foretaste of the grace that is necessary in order to secure a place at the heavenly banquet.

Just as no text should be twisted out of its context and pressed into foreign service, interpretation is limited when drawn from images of another time.[21] We do not "have the eyes to see" all that the eyewitnesses of the fifteenth century perceived in this doctrine of Double Intercession. What does clearly remain to be seen, however, is the parallel position of Mother and Son, breast and side, milk and blood. This is a eucharistic scene, depicting a vivid image of the sacrament of sacrifice. It involves the believer in "seeing double," male and female participation in the work of intercession and the nourishment of faith.

But what, if any, current illumination of the sacrament can be drawn from this illuminated manuscript from the middle-age of Western Christendom? This image vividly invokes some of the arguments for the Reformation: a blasphemous equalization of Mother and Son, the withholding of the cup from the laity, a reliance on image instead of Word for worship. Whatever this image may have meant to women in the past, there seems to be no place for it at our sacramental tables now.

In addition to this Protestant voice of protest is a feminist critique of Christianity's "normalization" of human suffering as redemptive.[22] Is the image of wounded son and pleading mother suspect theologically *and* ethically? Are these open wounds and exposed breasts too abused or exposed to be holy? Perhaps iconoclasm, "destroying of image," is in order?

But, what if this image represents historical evidence for an intimate relationship between women and eucharist that possesses social power, a *theoria* that could redeem a distortion of our self-image?[23] Female breasts no longer function as primary *religious* symbols of food in this culture that is over-stimulated by sexual imagery. Both food and body are products for Market, not religious symbols. Can a woman's body communicate sacramental meaning? Can a woman's body "mean" a human body? If we are used by our culture and its image-makers to symbolize the profane with our bodies, can we denounce that profanity and choose to interpret our bodies as signs of all that is holy and human? Socially constructed realities can suffocate. What is needed is the in-breaking breath of the Spirit.

At-One-Ment and Atonement

"This is my body" I say at the table filled with students thinking about Women and Worship. The cup and loaf are on the table as I recite the gospel narrative, the Words of Institution. "Is this your body?" I ask. There is a long silence. "Is your body-blood also *his* body-blood?" There is a longer silence. Then, "Not literally," one finally ventures. "There is a spirit connection, not body," another offers. "AT-ONE-MENT" is the verbal solution applied to their curious silence. With this word, these *imago Christi* women recover their voices, and find permission for themselves to be at the table.

Why such initial resistance to our at-one-ment of body and blood? Why not face-to-face? We see our *imago Christi* reflection in a cracking mirror; we see ourselves through the wavy distortions of time. Many of us turn our eyes away from mirrors, avoid reflection, duck out from under a concentrated focus on our outline, motives, methods. There is little delight in what we see, our image is not insight.

(One curious statistic from the Women's Action Coalition sticks out in this bricolage of women, food, and grace: Thirty thousand American women underwent the procedure of liposuction in 1991, and surgeons sucked 200,000 pounds of body tissue from them.[24] This single statistic makes a rude sucking noise I can't explain away.)

What forms of worship would empower us to claim *imago Christi* in a female shape? Does female experience leaven the loaf and its meaning? Is the natural curve of a chalice and the curve of a breast only a surface impression? Does the eucharist carry a taste of gender?

"To the medieval natural philosopher, breast milk was transmuted blood, and a human mother—like the pelican that also symbolized Christ—fed her children from the fluid of life that coursed through her veins."[25] Nursing images from the natural world spilled over into sanctuary statues, stained glass, icons, manuscript illustrations. The link between Christ's body and Mary's breast is clearly expressed in medieval images. It is absent from the modern view.

The human body as holy food is an ancient symbol in

humanity's self-expression. Clement of Alexandria provides one of the oldest sources of the Eucharist where the newly baptized are served milk and honey, bread and wine.[26] For Clement, the Logos, the Word, was milk for the believer. The image of the church as a nursing mother was common; so was the understanding of blood as the raw material of all life.[27] By joining the biblical texts of 1 Corinthians 3:1-3 to John 6:51-55, the early church understood itself to be fed with nurturing male and female images in the holy meal of Christ. Milk, blood, birth, and body are the strong raw symbols with which we can, like our medieval sisters, re-form our lives of worship.

Bread of Life: Baking and Making Holy

For many women the at-one-ment with Christ and the Spirit is located not in the cup but in the bread. This connection between bread and body is reinforced by a gender role of food provider-preparer. The historical association of women's altar guilds and their preparations for communion make this connection appear more "natural" for worshiping communities. Body transformed to bread does not appear to "frighten" or alienate to the same degree as body to cup.

But when the image of woman (human) as bread is extended to woman (baker) as God, friction is created. "Warm" denominational discussions were held over the liturgical use of the image of Bakerwoman God from Alla Renée Bozarth's poem.

>*Bakerwoman God*
>
>Bakerwoman God,
>I am your living bread.
>Strong, brown, Bakerwoman God,

I am your low, soft and being-
shaped loaf.
I am your rising
bread, well-kneaded
by some divine and knotty
pair of knuckles,
by your warm earth-hands.
I am bread well-kneaded.
Put me in fire, Bakerwoman God,
put me in your own bright fire.

I am warm, warm as you from fire.
I am white and gold, soft and hard,
brown and round.
I am so warm from fire. . . .[28]

Many religious women in grain-based cultures view the baking of bread as a necessary process for a whole and holy meal. Baking may also function as a tangible form of *anamnesis,* the re-membering which makes the past and the future present. Jesus took bread and blessed it, but there were other hands which kneaded and pressed it. Is their presence discerned or rendered invisible in the substance of that which is broken and shared in worship?

Women who are deeply engaged in the spiritual leadership of a worshiping congregation often express this "deepening of ordinary human experience" as the source of the holiness of the meal.

Yet, food is not merely our primordial need; it is also our primordial pleasure. A theology of food reminds us not only that our lives are precarious, dependent on mysterious sources of sustenance which we cannot clearly control. . . . Even as I write this paragraph, I am in the process of baking shortbread for a friend whose husband is ill. The house is rich with the smell of butter, subtly scented with almond extract. Such smells call vividly to mind (No: not just to mind; to embodied mind, to fleshly mind) that life as God's gift is not about *mere* being.[29]

Human breadmaking has held holy meaning since the first domestic uses of grain. It is a natural symbol in those cultures that are grain-fed. "Blessed art thou, O Lord our God, who bringest forth bread from the earth" is an ancient blessing of God for the creation of bread. It states a conviction, shared by Jews and Christians, that the "making" is a means of sharing in the holiness of creation. This sharing in the holiness of creation is also connected to the symbolic power of rice, which is re-forming the sacramental awareness of many Asian Christians.

> In Korea, for instance, Christian feminist groups have formed a Women-Church that has operated since 1989 and has a pastor who coordinates its twice-weekly services. . . . As the women gather they celebrate an agape meal of rice and chilled ginger tea in remembrance of Jesus' table hospitality with the outcasts of his society.[30]

The narrative of the presence of bread at the table of the upper room supplies evidence of the presence of the women who were friends and disciples of Jesus. Historical images and texts can be used to deny women's presence in the table fellowship of Jesus in order to maintain their absence in the present. Does the tangible evangelism of bread, expressed and experienced through time, make real the presence of women who worship?

Real Presence

Without help of texts or benefits of context, women pass the bread of life from hand to hand. Bread has been a woman's form of art, which tastefully undermines the visual dominion of an all-male Supper. The holiness and the humanness of this meal, however, is not dependent on a gendered division of labor. Nostalgia is not the goal of a worshiping community. Holiness and humanness resides in the presence of the Spirit and the interconnectedness of a particular community's everyday life and liturgy. The Bread of life involves both the baking and making of holiness within a community of worshiping women and men.

Some women refuse to come to communion because they are disconnected from this "making of holiness" by an interiorized shame. Long after the powerful exchange of the Syrophoenician woman and Jesus (Mark 7:24-30) has become glossed over, worn down to expected pleasantries, the question remains: Who is worthy? One theological answer states that no one is worthy. But when a woman responds, "We are not worthy / so much as to gather up the crumbs"[31] because socioeconomic and psychological structures teach her that, our theology must take issue with that answer. It is clear that this prayer response has lost the fierce scriptural grip of a mother who wouldn't let go of Jesus or turn loose of the table. We need more of the force of Ada Maria Isasi-Diaz's *abuelita*, a grandmother who used to say, "A Dios rogando, y con el mazo dando [Pray to God at the same time that you strike with the hammer]."[32]

Worthy, Yes, Worthy!

The call comes as I am reaching for the first of many boxes just unloaded in the parsonage dining room. Someone's mother is in intensive care. Mixed between the adult words of a daughter is the sound of a frightened child. I promise an immediate departure and consider my options as I search for the suitcase with suitable clothes. I have been in the community less than a day. The reported response to my presence ranged from anxious to angry. The unknown parishioner is in critical condition. She has just turned eighty, "belongs" but does not attend church, and has children who are Roman Catholic. I scan for hose without holes as I open the box marked "Altar."

The someone's mother is small and made smaller by the tubes, trays, and screens. I say her name and her eyes focus and then wander. I say her name again, then start the Lord's Prayer. Her lips move, but no sound. I name her again and ask if she wants communion. I read the slight pressure of her fingers as assent and begin to prepare her "Last Supper." I feel a reluctant gratitude for the ever-ready wafers. I dip one in the cup and place it carefully on her dry tongue. The prayers are said, keeping a careful eye on the wafer, which I remove after "Amen." I wipe her forehead and mouth with a moistened cloth, say her name again, and leave to find her family.

Only after we are deep in conversation about her condition does my choice of pastoral care turn risky. A loud silence crashes down as I share the news of communing their mother. Glances are exchanged and brows lifted, but no one translates. I make several attempts to repair the breach but finally succumb to a parting prayer and an exit. I barely clear the corridor before the commentary starts behind me.

It took four days for the meal to go public. I had, depending on the source, either committed a mortal sin or performed a miracle. The woman whom I had led to the bedside table had never walked to an altar in the memory of the community. What I had assumed would stir old memories had broken the habits of a lifetime of restraint. To some of her connections, I had force-fed a dying woman and threatened her salvation. To others, I had offered their beloved friend and mother the bread of life. To the inscrutable will and whimsy of God belonged the verdict: the dying woman didn't die.

She recovers. She recovers her appetite and then her energy. She returns home and then returns to church. She refuses to use the handicapped entrance, preferring to go hand-over-hand up the steep stairs.

She sits in the notoriously empty front pew, close, very close to the table. Whatever crippling sense of unworthiness she has suffered is gone. Whatever has divided her body from the body of Christ has disappeared. She believes, as few do, in the *real presence* of Christ. She is present for that presence. She teaches me in body language something about a doctrine I don't believe: transubstantiation.

All the classic descriptions of the Eucharist can be observed in her table manner. This sacrament is the locus of joy, assurance, union with Christ, thanksgiving, sacrifice, communion, and mystery. She experiences herself as being worthy to be fed, is assured of being loved, yet recognizes her daily need for forgiving grace.

To Eat to Our Own Damnation

Women hunger to create and maintain a distinctive self-identity. Their own bodies become the means to this end. Unlike medieval women, modern women fast not for the purposes of salvation, but for self-identity. "Anorexia can be understood as a pathology of reflexive self-control, operating around an axis of self-identity and bodily appearance, in which shame and anxiety play a preponderant role."[33] One liturgical implication that seems directly connected to this issue of shame and self-control is the reluctance that some women clergy have to eat "in front" of others even when they serve communion.

The early Christian communities were cautioned against the failure "to discern the body," which meant a failure to recognize the presence of Christ in their table fellowship. This first-century failure to discern Christ's body has a twentieth-century counterpart: we, as women, fail to discern *imago Christi* in our bodies.

Failure to discern the body, *imago Christi,* in ourselves and in creation leads to a damning form of starvation. The Market feeds our growing hunger for the symbolic power of body and food relationships. It extends control issues from our selves to our shelves. Even those of us who view commercials with a hermeneutic of suspicion admit being moved to tears by a 30-second McDonald's spot.[34] Our hunger for true table fellowship lures us into deep-fried sentimentality.

Media images of feeder and fed have redesigned the traditional female apron strings so that they can encompass the commercial girth of Ronald McDonald, Wendy's dad, and the Dunkin' Donuts man. Women's private sphere of kitchen and nurture has gone public, and that public, now-profitable sphere is populated by male figures.*

---

* A warning to the reader: the "tone" of this section becomes "strident," one of the consistent critiques of women's writing as pointed out by Carolyn G. Heilbrun, *Writing a Woman's Life.*[35] The flashpoint anger I feel when confronted with the Dunkin' Donuts man comes from my memory of my grandmother and her doughnuts. She was the one who labored endlessly, strove to feed every hunger, suppressed her own desires . . . and here my deeper anger bubbles away like hot grease. "Nostalgia, particularly for childhood, is likely to be a mask for unrecognized anger."[36]

Some of our mothers and grandmothers were confined to not-for-profit kitchens by the gender divisions of an industrialized marketplace. Some of our sisters continue to labor long hours in

One graphic proof of this culture's willingness to consume women's experience in profane ways is *Silence of the Lambs*. The film's antihero is a male psychiatrist who "did lunch" with some of his clients. The villain is a victim, a child-abused killer who specializes in skinning young women. Its nerve-racking narrative alternates between these men and the young women they "consume." The doctor feeds on the emotions and memories of a young female officer. The killer cages his prey until her body is ready for skinning. They share an abused male's ravenous hunger for the intimacies of a woman's life. They are willing to destroy the human life and dignity of individual women in order to get inside the generic skin of female experience.

This cannibalism of the female body is not limited to a technologically advanced culture. Peggy Reeves Sanday in her work *Divine Hunger and Cannibal Monsters: Cannibalism as a Cultural System* describes a range of cultures where there is a link between cannibalism and the use of the female body as symbol.[37]

Contrast this narrative with the ones found in the Gospels. The victim is not trapped like an animal or rendered less than human. "I lay down my life for my friends." The offer of body is made even when it is clear that his life will be forcibly taken. The violence which crucifies is not portrayed as normal human behavior. It violates human and holy law. The liturgical *anamnesis* of this narrative, which begins with a meal and ends with the promise of a banquet, offers opposition to this culture's unholy hunger, its cannibalism of all who are "weaker."

---

the Market *and* are on permanent kitchen duty. When this moustached corporate caricature of the working poor peddles doughnut holes on national TV, I react as if I am being force-fed the idolatrous meat of the apostle Paul's marketplace.

In *Holy Feast and Holy Fast,* Caroline Bynum details an earlier world of Christian formation and gender identity which revolved around the altar-table. Her study demonstrates that medieval men and women inhabited the same house of language and culture, but they selected vastly different symbolic surroundings. Women chose certain symbols such as eating, acts of relationship, and suffering more frequently than men. One implication that can be drawn from her study is the necessary relationship of fast to feast. To refrain from consumption was not an act of self-hate, it was an act of protest against the ravenous demands of the world.

Postmodern women and men inhabit the same universe, yet seemingly live in different worlds of meaning. A sacrament, by its nature, is multivalent. There is one meal, but many meanings. There is body, blood, bread, and wine, but the means of receiving of this sameness may differ.

> They [men and women] used symbols in different ways.
> Men, who were dominant, used symbols (among them
> the male/female dichotomy) to renounce their domi-
> nance. Reversals and oppositions were at the heart
> of how symbols worked for men. . . . To women, how-
> ever . . . symbols of self were in general taken from bio-
> logical or social experience and expressed not so much a
> reversal or renunciation of worldly advantage as the
> deepening of ordinary human experience that came
> when God impinged upon it.[38]

Table Manners

The order of a communion service is changing, and it may be due to the shift in gendered roles. We are witnessing a reversal of the feeding order. A noticeable increase of pastors serve the elements to the congregation first and then serve themselves last. Does this "turning the table" indicate that the cultural relationship of women to food is reversing itself? Can the change be seen as the further feminization of the role of clergy; that is, serve first, then eat?

When I interviewed men and women pastors who feed others first, I perceived a shift in the role of pastor toward that of "host." Good hosts feed guests first. The presider is clearly responsible for table hospitality. Add to this hosting table manner the gendered custom of women serving others first. The relationship of women and their table labor will surely be affected when a woman's hand is at the altar as the server. These are ceremonial manners, which assume a significance in the world as well as in the sanctuary. If the liturgical dichotomy of males as givers of food and females as receivers is dissolving, the act of *receiving* and serving can take on a new significance.

Marietta Holley, a nineteenth-century American humorist, attempted to "altar" her context of women, work, and worship. In her satire *Samantha among the Brethren*, early Methodist women sweat as they labor to repair the interior of the Meeting House while the men stand by and inform them that "The Methodist Conference (1888) had decided that wimmen wuz too weak to set," that is, attend the meetings as elected delegates. While piety indeed appeared to have become the private property of Protestant women, it required a careful ownership. Women were to avoid leadership in worship, yet stretch their personal influence for holiness under the direction of men, who controlled the rites and rights of worship.

Wall, we wuz all engaged in the very heat of the war-fare, as you may say, a-scrubbin' the floors, and a-scourin' the benches by the door, and a-blackin' the 2 stoves that stood jest inside of the door. We wuz workin' jest as hard as wimmen ever worked—and all of the wimmen who wuzn't engaged in scourin' and mappin' wuz a-settin' round in the pews a-workin' hard on articles for the fair—when all of a suddin the outside door opened and in come Josiah Allen with 3 of the other men brethren.

They had jest got the great news of wimmen bein' apinted for Deaconesses, and had come down on the first minute to tell us. . . . And Josiah wanted me to know immegietly that I, too, could have had the privi-lege if I had been a more single woman, of becomin' a deaconess, and have had the chance of workin' all my hull life for the meetin' house, with a man to direct my movements and take charge on me, and tell me what to do, from day to day and from hour to hour . . .

I, myself, took the news coolly, or as cool as I could, with my temperature up to five or five and a half, owin' to the hard work and the heat. But Miss Sypher is such a admirin' woman, she looked fairly radiant at the news, and she spoke up to her husband in her enthusiastik warm-hearted way—

"Why, Deacon Sypher, is it possible that I, too, could become a deacon, jest like you?"

"No," sez Deacon Sypher solemnly, "no, Drusilly, not like me. But you wimmen have got the privelege now, if you are single, of workin' all your days at church work under the direction of us men."

"Then I could work at the Deacon trade under you," sez she admirin'ly, "I could work jest like you—pass round the bread and wine and the contribution box Sundays?"

"Oh, no, Drusilly," sez he condesendinly, "these hard and arjuous dutys belong to the male deaconship. That

75

is their own one pertickiler work, that wimmen can't infringe upon. Their hull strength is spent in these duties, wimmen deacons have other fields of labor, such as relievin' the wants of the sick and sufferin', sittin' up nights with small-pox patients, takin' care of the sufferin' poor, etc., etc. . . . I would not wish for a moment to curtail the holy rights of wimmen. I wouldn't want to stand in her way, and keep her from doin' all this modest, unpretendin' work for which her weaker frame and less hefty brain has fitted her."[39]

Feasting in an Age of Fasts

"The holy rights of wimmen, all this modest, unpretendin' work." Is it possible for worshiping women to hold love of life and suffering together at the same table? Does the doctrine of atonement carry a side effect which is toxic to women's well-being? Caroline Bynum writes: "These symbols [wounded body, offered breast] enabled women to express and give meaning to certain basic realities that all societies face: the realities of suffering and the realities of service and generativity."[40] What are the symbols that express today's realities of suffering, service, and generativity?

Her nametag reads "Bonnie." I meet her in my first week on the job of truckstop chaplain. Hospitality is obvious in the way she serves your table. You are not an interchangeable part; you are an invited guest. I watch her for liturgical clues for my own service at the communion table.

Whenever she takes her break, we sit at the off-duty station and talk. She enjoys the idea that we are "doing theology." We have known each other for several months when her table talk changes. She inspects her own words as if they are cracked or dirty. Voices other than her own seem to break into her narrative.

I notice an increasing intensity about her service, an other-focused look to her body. She doesn't need a break. She takes on extra shifts. She covers others' tables. She is doing it all.

I ask her to sit and talk one evening. She reluctantly agrees to sit down. She breaks the restless silence by telling me about her first Bible. It was white leather and had her name written inside. She'd gotten it as a child from her church.

Bonnie seems to remember that her mother had played the piano for church. Her brothers and sister, eight in all, would line up and walk to Sunday school. Being poor means that they walked; it also means that it had been an adventure.

She and her twin brother, Donnie, would head the line, holding hands. The year they turned five, the Sunday adventure turned tragic. On the way home from church, a car rounded a corner too fast. One twin was taken and one was left.

She felt her twin being pulled from her hand. She tried to hold tight, but . . . (and here the grown woman twists a napkin into a knot) small fingers are no match against the grip of death. He died. She didn't. She remembers standing at his grave. She either remembers or imagines, the difference doesn't matter, that her mother refused to look at her and said, "Why him and not you?"

From that moment on, she had no name. She was simply called "Seven." On her first day of school, she was shamed when the teacher asked, "What is your name?" She said, "Seven," and wondered why they laughed.

Her little white Bible was a treasure; her name was

written there. But the family no longer walked to church. Once the preacher came to visit with his wife. They offered to adopt Bonnie. Her mother's anger was loud, dangerous. Bonnie first hid the knives and then herself in the kitchen. Her mother threatened to kill the preacher if he and his "stick of a woman" ever came back on her porch.

Bonnie went looking for her Bible at bedtime, the one with her name written inside the pretty white cover. She looked for days. Every day she'd come home from school and look for her book with her name. Nearly a month later, she found it, lying in the bottom of the apple cellar. And she knew, seeing it, that her mother had thrown it there.

She climbed down and picked it up and . . . (there follows a long silence at the table). "And . . . ?" I ask. "Oh, it wasn't any good anymore. The rats ate the leather, the rain washed my name away."

The next week she isn't at her station. The manager gives me the address, a mental institution, and shrugs off an explanation. "Oh, she stopped taking her medicine and thought Jesus had healed her."

When I enter the ward, she is sitting on her bed, one bed among other beds in one room. She has a Bible pressed against her heart. "I'm getting better," she assures me. "I am. It won't be long. But, you know, every day that I walk around holding the Bible, they write it down. I know it looks crazy, carrying it around. But the last time I was in here, I put my Bible in this little stand. See, there's no lock. Last time I was here, one of the really crazy women tore my Bible up. I just need to carry it around a few days more, then I'll be able to put it down. And they'll write on my chart that I'm getting better."

I walk her toward the dining room. It is supper time. "Do you know," she said, "most of these people here aren't crazy. They're just old and their families don't want them. They're just left over. Leftovers. I wish I had money. I'd build a nice place, I could take care of left-over people."

I stand at the door of the dining room. They wouldn't let me go in. "Crazy" people eat in that dining room. I watch Bonnie cross the room and sit down beside an old woman who is tied to her chair. Her head is moving without meaning; but her moans are perfectly clear. Bonnie reaches out to this empty face, and turns her head so that they are eye-to-eye. Then she picks up a spoon and begins to feed her supper.

I stand at the threshold marked "Sane" and watch a woman serve a messianic banquet with the elegance of a liturgy. Here is the table fellowship of leftover people. A waitress, a worthy woman, is spoon-feeding grace to a crazy old world. This is a table manner by which all sacramental practice can be judged. This is feasting in an age of fasts.

The Quilters

Blessed be the tie that binds:
   the heart
   the kindred mind
   the tear
   the inward pain
   the hope
   to meet again.

They are were always:
   frontier followers
   pioneers in Jesus
   quilters of the call.

They gather in:
   night and noon
   scraps of shadows
   snippets of light.

To gossip for God:
   stitch story skin
   quilt with gutstring
   unravel proud possessions of sound.

Tracing the grace:
   newly born
   freshly wed
   children's children
   treasured dead.

Wearing only thimbles
   quilters of the Call
   piece
   the four-square gospel
   crossXstitch
   truth in time.[1]

T H R E E

GOSPEL GOSSIP

But on the first day of the week, at early dawn, they
came to the tomb, taking the spices that they had prepared. They found the stone rolled away from the tomb,
but when they went in, they did not find the body.
While they were perplexed about this, suddenly two
men in dazzling clothes stood beside them. The women
were terrified and bowed their faces to the ground, but
the men said to them, "Why do you look for the living
among the dead? He is not here, but has risen. Remember how he told you, while he was still in Galilee, that
the Son of Man must be handed over to sinners, and be
crucified, and on the third day rise again." Then they
remembered his words, and returning from the tomb,
they told all this to the eleven and to all the rest. Now it
was Mary Magdalene, Joanna, Mary the mother of
James, and the other women with them who told this to
the apostles. But these words seemed to them an idle
tale, and they did not believe them. (Luke 24:1-11)

Under Suspicion

Quilting is, by tradition, communal. Women circle the
four corners of the quilting frame, stitching together

layers of cloth and conversation. This tradition provides multiple images of the relationship of women and Word. Like women gathered around the quilt frame, the community circles four corners of interpretation which anchor their work on the Word: suspicion, proclamation, remembrance, and creative actualization.[2]

Suspicion seems a strange place to begin a working relationship of women and Scripture. Suspicion normally unravels relationship, prevents the building of ties which bind. But there is ample biblical justification for a cautious interpretative approach to "the Word," as this passage from Luke reveals. The female friends of Jesus have experienced a close encounter with two of the heavenly host. Their witness, however, is received by the apostolic establishment as gossip, not gospel. Even the word "gossip" doesn't carry the weight of this apostolic disdain. Perhaps a weekly tabloid's lead story, such as "ALIENS INVADE GRAVE OF LOCAL RELIGIOUS LEADER," comes closer to expressing the suspicions the men had about the women's good news.

The phrase translated "idle tale" does not refer to casual conversation, or a trivializing of meaning, or even an exaggeration of experience. This resurrection story is described as women's non-sense, hysterical mouthing off, wild, homeless muttering.[3] A suspicious attitude toward women's revelation on the part of first-century religious authorities is preserved in this passage. Being placed under suspicion is a challenge contemporary women need to answer through critical study and careful interpretation of the relationship of text and context.

We, modern readers, and Christian believers, know that these grand mothers of faith got their story straight. Why such a curious twist to this Gospel? Apostolic teaching handed on this written tradition of disbelief by the church's first fathers. One entangling effect of this story of disbelief is the devaluing of women who have gospel encounters to share.

Jane Schaberg addresses this knotty text in her essay on Luke found in *The Women's Bible Commentary*. The story of the suspicious disciples is not just a loose end, an unfinished plot in the women's Gospel. Their recorded disbelief turns into a slipknot, which the early church used to rein in the witness of women.

> First, the impression of many women in this Gospel is conditioned by expectations of finding none or very few and by the impression, documented by psychologists, that numbers of women in mixed groups seem (to both men and women) much larger than they actually are.[4]

There are ten women named in the Gospel of Luke. Ten women with names, compared with one hundred and thirty-three men. Gospel women are to be hearers of the Word, but Luke never records their "doing" of the Word with the power and authority to teach and preach.[5] Some present-day successors to the apostles read and reach the same conclusion: faith is not connected to women's hearsay.

> The point seems instead to be that the faith of the men who are Jesus' successors is not based on the word of women, on indirect testimony. Nor is it based on the empty tomb: Peter verifies that it is empty, but the sight creates amazement, not faith. . . . Rather, in this Gospel, faith that Jesus has been raised is based on appearances and teaching of the risen Lord: to Simon [24:34], to the two disciples going to Emmaus [24:31], to the Eleven and their companions [24:41-43, 46, 52]. But in Luke the risen Jesus does not appear to women. Their witness is not essential to the Christian faith.[6]

We need to consider the dangers of plunging into a religious context that offers a glorified, gendered role to women. There are cautions to be observed whenever angelic messengers are overruled by "father knows best." If the communal witness of *imago Christi* women is forbidden in our *mundhaus* ("mouth-house"), Martin Luther's favorite word for church, then what is heard is not the Word truly preached. When the sound of women's religious experience is silenced, what is heard is not good news, but non-sense.

Nancy Woloch traces the American Protestant version of this apostolic disregard of women's witness. The historical situation of many nineteenth-century evangelical women has its Gospel parallel in Luke's narrative of Mary and Martha, the two sisters who were friends of Jesus. Mary's decision to sit at the feet of Jesus provided a model of contemplative life-style for Protestant women who had been cut off from women's traditions of spiritual authority such as those in Roman Catholicism. "In many ways, the evangelical Protestant experience was loaded with potential for women. Conversion encouraged introspection and self-attention. Cooperative efforts in church groups inspired a conscious sense of sisterhood and mutual interest. And clerical assurance of moral superiority supported a new degree of authority over others."[7]

This clerical assurance of women's moral superiority carried social force until American Protestant churches began to suffer from the separation of church and culture. A certain redemptive irony can be found in the clerical assumption of women's natural spirituality. Certainly the early church fathers would have been dismayed as church women began to slip out from under knotty texts which designated them hearers of the Word and nurturers of the men who are its doers. The bargain between clergy men and women parishioners depended upon women keeping their proper place.

> But religious activism also had built-in limitations; clerical support meant clerical control. In the heat of revivals, as female piety assumed new significance, ministers warned women to avoid the leadership roles as, for example, revivalists. Their piety was to be limited to the private role of personal persuasion; "influence" was contingent on acceptance of limits.[8]

This implicit bargain depended on keeping Martha in the kitchen and Mary on the porch, and both of them in some tension with their choices. Any woman, therefore, who kept to her "proper place," a church publication explained in 1823, could exercise "almost any degree of influence she pleases."[9] To the Marthas belonged the immense responsibility of local church nurture and the economies of mission. To the Marys belonged the receptive spirituality which would sustain the evangelical work of the male clergy. But what if Martha laid down her towel, and Mary got up to proclaim what she'd seen?

J. M. Buckley's 1888 address to the Methodist Centennial Conference, "What Methodism Owes to Women," articulates the necessity of keeping nineteenth-century church women in their place. He fiercely defended the right of the General Conference of 1888 to refuse to seat the laywomen who had been duly elected delegates from their annual conferences.[10] Yet, the firm foundation of properly displaced women began to shake as gender assumptions in church and culture underwent the earthquake called Twentieth-century.

I shall speak, therefore, of the ordinary work of women in Methodism. They constitute two-thirds of the membership. They furnish the largest numerical attendance on its means of grace. From them come the greatest number and the greatest average fidelity of Sabbath-school teachers. It is they whose voices furnish a large part of the music of the Church, and in many places without them there would be as little music in Methodist congregations as among the societies of Friends. The class-meeting, that peculiar institution of Methodism which in its best estate is unequaled in power for edification, encouragement, and guidance, and at its worst estate is a skeleton which in the time of revival suddenly becomes clothed with flesh and filled with warm blood, owes its power and perpetuity very largely to women.[11]

At the end of his accolade, he cautions women against the "danger of yielding to the solicitations of restless spirits to seek a degree and kind of prominence, the sure effect of which will be to drive those not of a masculine spirit into the background."[12] Lydia Maria Child, a church woman writing in 1841, predicted the effect that this separate, and not equal, ministry would have on evangelical societies. They had "argued upon women their prodigious influence and consequent responsibility," said Child. "They have changed the household utensil into a living energetic being."[13]

Whatever Luke's original purpose of the story of Mary and Martha, American church women rewrote the script of this scripture and emerged as living energetic beings with household utensils, and the gospel well in hand.[14] Women's voluntary associations were centers of social and ecclesiastical reformation. It was difficult to sustain the barriers between the private and public spheres of women's communication.

Records of the Nazarene Church reveal an alternative approach to the private and public spheres of women's communication. On September 15, 1853, the Reverend Luther Lee preached the ordination sermon of Antoinette Brown. His text was Galatians 3:28, but the context of his sermon was the radical discipleship of a holiness community composed of women and men called to proclaim the gospel.

> I do not believe that any special or specific form of ordination is necessary to constitute a gospel minister. We are not here to make a minister. It is not ours to confer on this our sister a right to preach the gospel. If she has not that right already, we have no power to communicate it to her. Nor have we met to qualify her for the work of the ministry. If God and mental and moral culture have not already qualified her, we cannot, by anything we may do by way of ordaining or setting her apart.[15]

By 1950, however, this narration had shifted from "we have always ordained women" to "we haven't forbidden them." But the clarity of God's call to women to the preaching of the gospel remains audible, even in the confines of their culturally appointed place. From *The Preacher's Magazine:*

"The Women's Sphere"

> Our church has never forbidden women to enter the ministry. It would be honest for us all to confess that such work has not been encouraged, but we are all convinced that God still calls women to be preachers of the gospel.[16]

Women may be trained to keep a proper silence in the sanctuary, but culture demands that they become bilingual in daily speech, capable of interpreting and speaking male and female language.[17] This bilingualness, required by culture, is part of the inspiration (in-breathing) of Spirit, which enables women to start the work of proclamation with *godsippe*, gossip.

Godsippe: the Voicing of God's Wisdom

The original meaning of gossip is *godsib*, the female friend who was present at the birth of a child, and who served as a godparent. *Gossiphood* referred to a spiritual relationship, a body of gossips.[18] The word carries an essential female sound, which has suffered a cultural profanity. The voicing of God's wisdom is a far cry from malicious rumor. But even when preaching was restricted to a males-only ministry, the "gossip" of the gospel went on. Now, reformative work on the word "gossip" returns it to its origin as *godsippe*, the voicing of God's wisdom.

The question of the *authority* of Scripture is a critical one for the task of voicing God's wisdom, but the *assumption of relationship* may be the primary issue. Do women conceive of Scripture as an objectifiable text, or as an active, articulate Presence? How does Scripture enter the sphere of women?

> When he came to Nazareth, where he had been brought up, he went to the synagogue on the sabbath day, as was his custom. He stood up to read, and the scroll of the prophet Isaiah was given to him. He unrolled the scroll and found the place where it was written. . . .
> (Luke 4:16-17)

Rebecca Chopp finds in the "gospel of women" a persuasive model of relationship and transformation which can become part of the tradition of women's *godsippe* and the proclaiming Word. In Luke 4:16-30, Jesus names and claims the presence of God, which transforms religious repression into liberating life.

> I will speak of this passage, for women can claim what they hear, and say what appears to them, in the power of the Spirit. To proclaim emancipatory transformation women are empowered to take back the Scriptures: to speak of them and to hear them, painfully, angrily, prophetically, hopefully, lovingly, and gracefully. In this manner Luke is especially helpful for he begins, as I hear the Word and words, by calling into question the very time, space, and identity of the order, and speaking for a very other place, a place of connection and rupture, of relations and hearing, a place which may be today the place of women.[19]

How can women-word relationship create a community of interpreters who attend to "the Word" not only in the amplified voice of tradition, but in the *godsippe* of women? Does careful attention to difference and detail render women's language incapable of cupping the grandeur of gospel?

Self-disclosure or Exposure

Preaching is a form of human speech that does not avoid the challenge of translating particular insights of personal experience into the common language of a community of faith. Caution signs, however, may need to be erected around uncritical use of women's experience. Traditional roles and relationships can pick up a negative undertone when used in sermons. Carol Norén describes sermon material that details women's relationships in ways that are detrimental for both preacher and congregation.

> When a woman preacher's self-disclosure or illustration about other women depicts women in relationship to others, gender stereotypes are reinforced more often than not. This seems to occur regardless of the theological or political viewpoint of the preacher, or the context in which the sermon is preached.[20]

What is the source of this fall from grace, this loss of favor? Norén locates part of the blame on women preachers who "attempt to cultivate intimacy or mutual vulnerability with the congregation. The stereotype being reinforced in such self-disclosure is that in relationships, women always want more."[21]

However, what if wanting more comes from a hunger for righteous relationships, a hunger which the Word of God creates? Does the fault lie in intimate *godsippe* or in a community that denies communion and persists in stopping up their ears? The vulnerability of Incarnation will always be offensive to self-defensive men and women. *Imago Christi* humans work to connect knowledge; they quilt pieces of separate knowing into complex patterns of communal perception. This hunger for an intimacy of word and world suggests that sermons create community when they engage a call-response pattern between preacher and people. But, *godsippe,* the sharing of God's wisdom, is not restricted to rhetoric. When words, actions, and images are "realized," consciously chosen to express reality, all language can be *imago Christi* body language.

The following example of *godsippe* is filled with the connectedness of women's bodies, and the humanness of time. This interview took place among four women in their late thirties and early forties. They have been members of the same church for at least ten years. With the exception of one, who is in theological school, they describe their vocational identity as "work outside the home."

L [interviewer]: Many churches, when a new baby comes into the family, they often put a rose on the altar. In the United Methodists' new *Book of Worship*, they offer prayers and some rituals for events that we often don't think about celebrating in church. For instance, there's a prayer for a newly engaged couple that could be said at an engagement party or in the church service if that's something they would share. Are there events that happen in your life that you would like to be able to celebrate in church and yet we don't currently have a ritual or way to do that?

D: I'm thinking of our kids and when we adopted the kids. That would have been wonderful to have been able to celebrate that at church.

L: Was there a rose on the altar or any kind of recognition? Announcement of the event? Do you remember?

D: I don't think so.

M: Was there any place you verbally . . . ?

D: I don't think there was any kind of celebration.

K: Like with the babies . . .

D: Now my friends did. My friends at the church and my friends outside the church had showers for us.

L: In your worshiping fellowship, there was no way to recognize it or honor it or celebrate it?

D: Ummm-mmm (no).

L: Can you think of other events that occur in your life?

M: Menopause! [instant laughter] I do think that we should . . .

D: Worship it!

L: What are we going to do to . . . I'm curious to know how you would recognize it? Celebrate it, grieve it, bitch about it?

M: Celebrate it! Celebrate it! I read an article that was wonderful about menopause! In ancient times, there was actual celebration.

L: There was a ritual for it.

M: You wore a crown in an all-day celebration. Now you no longer *are* the blood flow. You keep that wisdom within you.

K: Oh, no! [laughter]

M: You are no longer shedding that. This is a confirmation that now you have wisdom within you; you were at a new phase in your life.

L: Do you also now get a pew fan to . . . [a long period of laughter]

D: . . . to help you with the hot flashes! I can say that because earlier I was having hot flashes!

M: Now they're not hot flashes. You have to change the name, they're power surges.

D: Ooh! I like that. Well, M., the church *does* celebrate that. Only you have to be in the right group—at bell choir. [laughter] When I first started getting hot flashes, there were four of us, some because of hysterectomies, and some going through it naturally, but we would all sit there in our shirts [gesture], you know. So you have to be in the right group!

M: I know it's different. If there was some way that we could celebrate instead of, "Oh, god, she's now gone through all her life. She's in menopause. She's nothing!" Just really see it in a positive light.

K: Well, I don't know why age sixteen is so special to me, I haven't figured it out, because I didn't even drive when I was sixteen. But when my girls reached sixteen, I wanted to celebrate that, more than other birthdays. But I wanted to recognize it in church, and so I put sixteen roses on the piano. I feel like, I feel haughty, or whatever, that I shouldn't be doing that stuff, that I'm showing off or whatever, but, there are just certain things that are so special to me that I want everybody else to share in that.

D: I'll tell you what I would really like. I would like not only celebrations of graduation, or babies, or sixteenth birthdays. If I'm in worship on a Sunday morning, and I'm just really pleased because I saw a robin or my daffodils are blooming, I would love to be able to say that out loud. I don't think it's silly, but something that's simple.

Something that's simple. The longing for the celebration of the substance of a woman's body and life. Religious language which recognizes the glory of a daughter or a daffodil. But something simple can be easily dismissed as trivial. Is this gossip, not *godsippe?* Where is the rhetoric of a transcendent theological reality, or, put another way, will it preach? Can the language of women and worship go public in a pulpit, or is it properly confined to the choir loft? Marjorie Procter-Smith answers this question in *In Her Own Rite.*

God is perceived as present in and working through women's struggle for survival and dignity: in the particularity of women's experience which recognizes differences of race, class, age, culture; in experiences of embodiment, especially experiences coming from having women's bodies; in experiences of connectedness with all of creation; in the "tiny acts of immense courage" which are women's daily work; and in experiences of love of self as woman and of other women.[22]

Women continue to symbolize the body in this culture as Catherine Bell notes in *Ritual Theory, Ritual Practice*.[23] The images of the body, however, shift in value and symbolizing power. The female body is encouraged to variety by a culture that markets self-identity via labels. Within religious communities, however, the embodied language of women's experience is often discouraged within worship. This silencing of voice reduces worshiping women to the role of hearers, not doers, infants, not adults.

The word *infant* comes from Latin and means "unspeaking." Institutional forms of worship have participated in the infantilization of women's language and experience. But paradoxically, all proclamation arises from primal language. If a woman's naming of human-holy experience invokes our pre-oedipal connections, then recognition, not repression, is the answer. Unpacking "childish things" is a part of learning to express the Word of God in a mother tongue.

The semiotic body language of infant and mother underlies cognitive utterance, all forms of symbolic gesture and speech. Jean Wyatt's book, *Reconstructing Desire: The Role of the Unconscious in Women's Reading and Writing*, is illustrative.[24] Women poets remind us of the powerful forces of language and self-identity. As Marge

Piercy writes in "Unlearning to Not Speak," preaching, like poetry, is a form of human speech that risks primal connection:

> She must learn again to speak
> starting with I
> starting with We
> starting as the infant does
> with her own true hunger
> and pleasure
> and rage.[25]

Suspicion, proclamation, remembrance, and creative actualization are the corners of the quilted nature of women and the language of worship. The tie that binds all four corners is relationship; we find our place in the text and find our voice in our context. Women's language is "essentially embodied, passionate, relational, and *communal*."[26] Surely each of these descriptions applies to God's language as well: essentially embodied, passionate, relational, and communal.

The frequency of grandmother stories among church women points to a dynamic of inheritance, the transmission of *godsippe*, holy wisdom, by old women. In my own family, Mother taught us to be creative with the basic grammar of faith Grandma had instilled. In the end, all Grandma had left of a lifetime of King James and the language of daily life was the name "Mama," most of the 23rd Psalm, and the Baptist version of the Lord's Prayer with a curious twist to its end. "Forever and ever and ever and ever . . ." she'd pray and then language surprises would follow. Once as I tucked her in, she reached the forever part and then launched into "Humpty Dumpty sat on a wall, Humpty Dumpty had a great fall . . ." She paused, uncertain, "I don't remember the end of this prayer." My response was a hug and a silent prayer that I not outlive my language.

But as she returned to the forever part, seeking its proper end, I came to my senses, or *the* sense of her speech. I was hearing the sound of ancient synapses of grace. Someone had taught her nursery rhymes wrapped around the Lord's Prayer. Someone had held her while she was young and rocked those sounds deep into her consciousness. This was the drawstring of her identity, this intimate remembering of a woman and word. This was the work of worthy women, intent on fashioning a language of praise which would last a lifetime.

Creative Actualization

Part of proclamation comes from the human instinct and ability to make meaning, to symbolize. In the study of women's self-identity and ways of learning, the following pattern was noted among women who had found their voice and their value:

> Each learned to immerse herself in at least one symbol system from a very early age. This might have been music or art, but most often they found another world through books and literature. Frequently they kept a diary. Whatever the medium, as children these women were producers as well as consumers in the medium that they chose to develop.[27]

In the mid-1970s, the challenge of nonsexist language is issued in the classrooms and chapel of Duke University, as it is in most other mainstream seminaries. The volume and temperature of conversations in the halls are rising. It is time to engage in orthopraxis of worship.

So say women seminarians who were assisted in discernment by the prophetic ministry of Helen Crotwell, Duke University chaplain.[28]

Space is the first theological exercise. The dominant maleness of Duke's ironically understated "Chapel" is a visual exercise of Protestant erectitude, with a cigar-holding guardian of bronze in the foreground. But the shadowed interiority of the sanctuary encourages images of a maternal body. With a mixture of arrogant innocence and insight, a monthly mid-week "Nonsexist Service of Worship" is launched in the nave.

It is not the nave, exactly, but the chancel that we select for this work of women and worship. So accurately is this a reconstruction of Christendom's vaulting ethos, we fight against the impulse to whisper. We perch uneasily in the choir stalls, curbing the impulse to flee or flinch. We have a right and a rite to be there.

The printed prayers prove to be the easy part. Pronouns can be fixed. What about the domination of printed text on context? Our elaborate negotiations over leadership deconstruct tradition's decree, "Worship is necessarily hierarchical." Like the stonemasons, we chisel delicate balances of power and presence. How much granite? How much gravity? We labor over liturgies, knowing we do not work alone, but still we are isolated from the particularities of other women and their work of worship.

My particular assignment is proclamation for the second service. When I shift from what to how, I get stuck. Should I preach with or without notes? Should I ascend the steps of the stony pulpit and preach from its backside? Should I stand in the center of the chancel and direct the speech and silence of the gathered body like a choir? What would it take to preach female in a space that had historically and architecturally silenced the embodied voice of women?

This remembrance of things past now seems whimsical. "Nonsexist" has been revealed as a dysfunctional category. Now we have multiple texts of women's sermons; the shelves are lined with competing volumes of women's proclamation, biblical drama, and song. "Embodying the Word" is a standard phrase for homileticians. But I remember the painful absence of such ink, and the sharp-edged hostility of the masters of theology to new forms of preaching and prayer.

I go to the chapel for silence, for guidance, for language. The granite gravity of tradition crushes even the simplest of images. I cannot breathe, let alone think of preaching.

> Phrases of men who lectured here
> drift and rustle in piles:
> Why don't you speak up? [29]

This line from Marge Piercy's "Unlearning to Not Speak" names now what I couldn't name then. I retire to my bed, breathless from a real illness, pneumonia, and a constructed dis-ease. How to preach female? That question rests on another, how to be female, an *imago Christi* female? Into my head tumbled Mary and Martha with their unresolved quarrel. What would enable this text to bring peace, instead of create division in the household of freedom?

Unfinished business. This text is a razor-edged wall between worshiping women. I know this story by heart and by body. Even as a girl-child I knew it was not finished. Anyone who is a sister knows that when Jesus leaves town, there is going to be a god-awful fight in

Martha's house. Anyone who has a sister knows that rivalry for blessing does not break out in the street, but in the sacristy and the church kitchen.

I also know what I heard from the pulpit was not meant to be put into practice. Every sermon I'd ever heard denied Martha's worth as an *imago Christi* woman. She is compulsive, she is trapped in the easily ridiculed trivialities of female life, she lacks spiritual (substitute intellectual) ability. She commits the unpardonable sin of breaking silence and telling a holy man what to do. So who wants to grow up to be a Martha?

Elisabeth Schüssler Fiorenza's redemptive scholarship of Martha's role as *diakonia*, referring to eucharistic table service and ecclesial leadership, will be written a decade later.[30] Nevertheless, the subtext of women's reality remains untouched by any sermon. We knew, we *knew*, that if we practiced what we heard preached, we'd cancel the next church supper. No more bazaars, no more roast beef, no more missions or parsonage repair. Women's work appeared as a regrettable necessity in the preaching of this piece of gospel. How could this text be preached "female," freed from an oral tradition that fractures the household of faith and sets sister against sister?

Hearing into Life

Margaret P. Jones reflects on the historian's use of naming and language to construct knowledge. Recent work in oral histories displays a grace of language that preachers should practice. Knowledge, to a sociohistorian, is the knowing of relationships, a product of power, the cultural and social understandings that will be "agreed to." The historian's ear is tuned to relationships as they are narrated. This keenness of hearing, that is attention, is a primary requirement of the language of worship. "Loving attention aims at putting all its perceptions at the service of the one observed. Only the kind of attention that is born of nurturing love can confer the freedom and receptivity which enables the powerful listener to enter into every aspect of the subject's life."[31]

This historical approach of "loving attention" is the key to re-forming the painful divisions of Martha and Mary. I invite two other women to explore this unfinished narrative with the language of words and bodies. The image that suggests itself as the paradoxical form of preaching is dance, "the dance of Mary and Martha." It is a challenge to women, such as myself, who view our bodies as worthy only because of our capacity for work. To dance threatens control, suggests sheer pleasure in being.

> Martha-Mother.
> Martha-Mother.
> Ruler of pots and pans,
> brooms and schedules.
> There is starch in your sheets,
> your spine, and your world.
> There is even a right time for sneezes.[32]

The fundamental question which goes unanswered in scripture is whether these sisters, these worthy women, will be able to bless the *imago Christi* in one another. To reach that answer means that the three of us must explore the text with our skins, our memories, our muscular sense of what the truth might be. We give loving attention to our differences in order to discern if communion was possible. The creative actualization of this "bodying of Word" appears like a fragile structure on a page. When it was breathed, and danced within the congregation, a healing falls like balm on the word-wounds we suffer. We are sisters, worthy women. In the kitchen or the porch, we can be *imago Christi* for one another.

> To hold and be held.
> To sweep and to dance.
> To be blessed and give blessing.
> If communion happens here,
> if there is blessing here,
> there is hope we can be healed.
> Mary, bless us.
> Martha, bless us.
> In the name of Christ, we are one.[33]

Mother Tongue Trouble

There are references to female anatomy in scripture that convey dignity and recognition of women's *imago Dei*, but incorporating this biblical language in worship can prove difficult. The sentence, "From the womb of a woman, not the mouth of a man, your word will be born into time,"[34] is usually heard as an expression of female impertinence, not an affirmation of faith. Another example comes from Christina G. Rossetti's poem "In the Bleak Midwinter," which was written in 1872 and appeared first as a hymn in *The English Hymnal* of 1906. The third stanza is generally omitted:

> Enough for Him whom Cherubim
>   Worship night and day,
> A breastful of milk
>   And a mangerful of hay;
> Enough for Him whom Angels
>   Fall down before,
> The ox and ass and camel
>   Which adore.[35]

The silencing of the religious experience of women, a sin of omission, can be overcome by a community's willingness to discern and witness to *imago Dei* in women's lives and bodies. But there are powerful taboos which prevent this intimate connection between body and Word.

> It is, time and time again, God's Word that women are not allowed to represent. Why is it that women are not to speak in public of God, why is it a disgrace for women to represent God—except precisely that they present the physical body, and the relation of women's bodies to language, of language to bodies, of words to bodies in connections, in plurivocity, in openness, a relation of bodies and language against a Word that stands over, a Word that towers above?[36]

The issue of hearsay heresy is not limited to this domination of female religious expression. Language controls are exercised by a Market where men as well as women and children are seen as interchangeable objects. This Market language works to disembody the human self. Human desire is fine tuned into stimulus response. Our humanity is reduced to an impulse, and our freedom is consumed in the quest for a quality product. In place of relationships, we are offered corporate connections. We learn to mistrust our own body's seasons and our mortality. We are taught fear of the other, thereby denying whatever communion human *imago Dei* offers. "Should the language of worship grow more out of positive faith affirmations or negative anti-heretical statements? What are the heresies that are most dangerous for the church today; could racism, sexism, or idolatry be among them?"[37]

The root meaning of orthodoxy is "right practice," not

"right doctrine." When keeping a critical eye out for too-earthy prayers and inspecting liturgies for the mote of untraditional names for God, we may yet leave the beam of corporate sin in place. What is desperately needed is a community where a deepened hearing and speaking sense of Godself becomes a means of breaking silence. This is language worthy for worship. It subverts the structures of sin and openly calls us to the *weorthscipe* of God.

> The goal of worship is also to witness to the gospel of God's love made known in Jesus Christ and to call persons and communities into faithful discipleship. On the other hand, the goal of gender socialization is to maintain the present social system; thus it subverts the Christian freedom to respond to the call of God who "has brought down the powerful from their thrones and lifted up the lowly."(Luke 1:52)[38]

The rewards of *imago Christi* worship far outweigh the risks of breaking tradition's code of silence. The communal hearing of prophetic witness is a willing suspension of tradition's disbelief. It enables those who have gone unheard to regain their power of narrative, a source of identity. Here the layers of *weorthscipe* language are pieced together by the community: *the worthiness of God* as known through many women's experience of the Spirit, scripture, and community; the *worthiness of imago Christi women's forms of worship;* the *weorthscipe of women,* who are created *imago Dei.*

The power of language to create a sense of worth and a symbolic system is deeply attractive for women searching for value and voice. Research of women who "pieced the four-square gospel and crossXstitched truth in time" continues to re-form the written history of Christian preaching.[39]

Hearsay Heresy

When and where does a contemporary household of faith give a woman permission to speak "gospel" in public with authority? How is this authority withheld and by whom? What is the proper place for "wordy" women? Anyone who engages in a reformation of worship language, seeking for worthy forms of praise for *imago Christi* humanity, needs a good grasp of the history of heresy. Early Christian communities that gave voice to women's religious experience in worship were held in suspicion by the skeptical successors to the apostles. One group, named Marcus's Circle, stirred the ire of Irenaeus, an early church guardian of orthodoxy: "Prayers are offered to the Mother in her aspects as Silence, Grace, and Wisdom; women priests serve the eucharist together with men; and women also speak as prophets, uttering to the whole community what the 'Spirit' reveals to them." [40]

Those who break the patriarchal order of silence and cross the boundaries between the Word and women's words are vulnerable to the accusation of unworthy behavior and speech. The communal language of Christian praise and prayer is largely ritual language. Any reformation of worship language must deal with three basic dynamics of ritual language: that it is what is expected, that it is assumed to be *the* truth, that "the ability to use the language correctly marks the user as a member of the community." [41] When an individual or a community explores other names for God, such as Mother, and engages in nonhierarchical actions such as sharing eucharistic authority, the charge of heresy can arise.

The power to name our holy-human relationships in worship cannot be casually exercised, because this is where reality, *truth*, is established for the community.

But when the community's sources of identity are changing, orthodoxy's boundaries can be overdrawn. A tight circle of creedal control expels rival versions of the oneness of God, and excommunicates true believers.

Any word of tradition that places women outside the circle, and under suspicion is unworthy of the Word of *imago Christi*. The suppression of Christian women's rightful relationship to the Word fractures the Word dwelling within and among us. "In this way the Word itself has suffered: Word has been separated, time and time again, from its fullness and denied its solidarity with creation (which it, after all, created as the bridge of chaos and order), its embodiment in incarnation, and its rhythm of resurrection and crucifixion."[42]

Where can a worshiping woman's ability "to signify" for a community receive confirmation instead of accusations of unorthodox behavior? Those who carry on "discourses of emancipatory transformation"[43] cannot simply talk to one another. Nevertheless, the risk of ecclesiastical backlash for worship and preaching that presses against the confines of convention is real. Gospel is easily turned into gossip, and hearsay can become heresy, as this footnote details.[44]

Awareness of the theological politics of women's religious experience is a necessary component of worship leadership. Women's *hearsay* of Christian faith can come under suspicion of heresy. The risk of articulating women's spiritual experience is not new. Female mystics such as Julian of Norwich had to submit their accounts of religious experiences to priestly guardians of orthodoxy. Having one's Easter witness condemned as "an idle tale" should not come as a surprise to us.

Worship reformation through nonsexist (the avoidance of gender-specific words), inclusive (the balancing of gender references), and emancipatory (transforming language) patterns[45] generates controversy in many congregations. Invocations of the Spirit without the standard trinitarian recitation is a criticism frequently directed toward feminist services, although this pattern occurs in many nondenominational worship patterns. Just as those in the early community of Marcus discovered, scriptural images of God as mother are heard as heretical when used in prayer.

Learning to Talk Earthy

Another radical reformation of worship language involves Christ and nature. Prayers for the earth can strengthen our recognition of the bond between our bodies, Christ's body, and the earth as the Body of God, but also leave room for critics to charge us with pantheism. Placing a cloth globe, circled with a crown of thorns, on the altar where the cross normally stands, may reform our theological concept of Christ and nature through a percept, a sense impression of an object.

To refuse to risk these connections in worship because they cannot be completely controlled by language produces a word-dominated form which denies image as insight. An act of worship esteems the being of an other. When the other is Earth, creation of God, we are not rejecting the tradition of the psalms, but re-forming that language into a new act of praise.

There are images of nature within our sanctuaries, but they are domesticated, pastel, very *unnatural*. We sing "In the Garden" but live "in the jungle," both ecologies distorted by human sin.[46] What theological insights might we gain if nature got a fair hearing in our prayers? Would we move so securely from confession to pardon if whales had the right to the rite of absolution? The Festival of St. Francis, held each October in New York City in the Cathedral of St. John the Divine, gathers up the orders of creation in a procession to the communion table. A young child carries a bowl of water with algae. An elephant follows a bishop, and both greet the worshipers on either side of the aisle with the same dignified nod of recognition. Whimsical? Perhaps, but it is God's fierce whimsy.

One vision of the young who suffer from our forcible separation of salvation and creation emerged in my own community. We have acquired new hymnals. Children old enough to read are encouraged to find a title they like and draw a picture of the song. I collect the drawings of smiling suns and Picasso people. One catches my eye. What *is* wrong with this picture?

One little girl, suspended between heaven and earth. One very sad little human whose tears are drawn from her head to her toes. What in the world is going on in the world of Phyllis, age eight? I check the number of the hymn for some kind of clue to this vision of despair. There it is, "Morning Has Broken," one of the celebratory songs of creation. What had produced this reversed image, this distortion? I lay her drawing beside the hymnal and then see what Phyllis, age eight, had seen. The sun, drawn between two mountains, has a crack from top to bottom. Morning has *broken*. This image has refused to fade. Each new statistic of a species' demise summons up the vision of Phyllis, age eight. What will reach the depth of this brokenness? How can a preached word filter into this pre-adult mind and offer both consolation and an opportunity to plant her feet firmly on this blessed earth and work for its preservation?

By Phyllis Baker   Morning has Broken
Pg. 145

Is the earth *imago Christi* now?[47] The image has troubling implications for those Christian theologians who caution against the imminent and immanental collapse of God and Nature. The image also imposes a sharp christological edge against the other religions of this blue-green world. With those profound limits in mind, however, the image continues to suggest itself as a vision that could begin the healing of the morning. If the earth could visually signify Christ's body, would it be possible to effect a transference through the liturgy between an image of the cross and the earth, without a distortion of *imago Christi*?

The earth and Christ. The standard image of the earth and the cross places the cross on top of the world. What would it mean to locate the cross within the world, a world wearing a crown of thorns? What reformation of prayer and action might result from turning the cross upside down, placing it *under* the earth? A heresy hunter might find this reversal idolatrous, since upending the traditional image produces the outline of the symbol for woman. There are, however, vital insights, *theoria* of the cross which can only be seen from down under.

The ecological threat to our continued created existence is not simply a matter of divided minds and bodies, or theologies that reduce the work of creation to a preamble and nothing more. We suffer from a paralysis of nerve. Young Phyllis had drawn the modern Christian dilemma very clearly. We are suspended, helplessly grieving between heaven and earth. We feel the disconnection from the structures of authority. We, the church, are not in charge. We sense the dangerous choices the adults (the principalities and powers of empire) are making, but we numb ourselves to the news.

Proclamation that empowers us to esteem the being of God, Christ, and the earth overcomes paralysis, regrounds those who want to be connected to communities of faith with working nerves. One dangerous temptation is to assume that liturgy is life. The second dangerous temptation is to deny that liturgy is life. Between these two temptations, we trace a delicate balance, engage a fragile ecological sphere of worshiping humans created *imago Dei.*

Forms of proclamation and prayers that resist our involvement with demonic structures of oppression, our flirtation with death are needed. Julian of Norwich, a worshiping woman from another time and place, offers her dream that is both liturgy and life.

> A little thing, the size of a hazel nut, in the palm of my hand, and it was as round as a ball. I looked at it with my mind's eye and I thought, "What can this be?" And the answer came, "It is all that is made." I marvelled that it could last, for I thought it might have crumbled to nothing, it was so small. And the answer came to my mind, "It lasts and ever shall because God loves it." And all things have being through the love of God. In this little thing I see three truths. The first is that God made it. The second is that God loves it. The third is that God looks after it. What is God indeed that is maker and lover and keeper. I cannot find words to tell.[48]

The gospel declares that principalities and powers that threaten what God has made, have already been overcome by the One incarnated, crucified, and risen. Enactments of earthy and earthly justice can take place within the sanctuary as a model for faithful witness beyond church walls. Christ's redeeming work of healing the morning requires the kind of proclamation, *god-*

sippe, that turns weapons into flower vases and lifts the crown of thorns off the brow of creation. We, all God's human creatures, need to be engaged in this Easter work of creative actualization.

Remembrance

One memory of a woman placed under suspicion has served as the tie that binds many of my pieces of gospel *godsippe* together. We are in the same preaching class. She is tall, a single mother of twin girls: "Very dark, but comely," is this "daughter of Jerusalem."

This woman's particularity of God, her struggle for survival and dignity, is a proclamation that offends and converts. I first hear her preach barefoot in the seminary Chapel. Her text is the fiery call of Moses. She takes off her shoes, for, she says, the space between God's people of any race, any class, any theology is holy ground.

She also takes off her shoes as a reminder of all children, like herself, who were forced to take turns wearing shoes in order to attend school. Her family could not afford a pair for each girl, so the sisters took turns. She moves then to the work of interpreting the text, and one by one, all over the chapel, men and women quietly remove their shoes.

Our first assignment for preaching class is to "walk around" the assigned text with a partner. The week before the moment of truth, we do exegetical work as a team. The class is highly charged, well motivated, to understate the situation. We believe that this is no academic exercise. Preaching is a class act that has direct bearing on our location and station in the real world of church. Talent here means power there.

My friend comes in on her assigned day, but does not claim the pulpit. She stands in the front and looks at each of us long enough to stir apprehensions. When she finally speaks, she is matter of fact. She has decided, she says, to invite us to tell the truth. Instead of hiding behind the pulpit where "no one knows if you fear God 'cause they can't see your knees," she stands in our midst and speaks her body and mind.

She has "walked around" this text, Mark 9:33-37, until she is tired, but the only word the Spirit gives her is "Walk around the text." She decides that all of us together have to take the journey. Instead of preaching on this troublesome passage about quarrelsome disciples and who is the greatest, she asks us to explain what it means for our preaching. We are to turn to our partner, take turns reading the text aloud, and then simply tell the truth about ourselves and this text. She will come and sit with each of us awhile and listen for the truth.

I remember staring at my fingers, terribly afraid for her and her "idle tale," this manner of gossiping about the gospel. I remember our discomfort on hearing this "Word." Anger, confusion, confession are articulated in this congregational "sermon." We, each in a personal way, try to tell the truth. As for my friend . . . she listens to each of us and fails the course in preaching. It is not the first theological course she has failed; but it is her last.

At the end of the year, she is encouraged to withdraw and consider her call. I walk her to the parking lot on the final day. When we reach the car, she announces, "I'm going to give you something." I fumble in my mind for a suitable response. Nothing turns up, so I simply extend my hand.

"It's a hard present. But I want you to keep it." She turns to face the stony outline of the chapel, and asks,

"What does it mean to succeed in an institution dedicated to the Suffering Servant?"

That is the gift. It has been a hard gift to keep. We stand for a moment eye to eye, then she sets out on her own gospel journey. She placed a question in my keeping and its hard grip has never loosened. Whatever the relationship is between *godsippe*, gospel and women, it is not just a matter of good preaching.

The Greek word *mysterion* refers to something on which silence must be kept. It is used to describe the sacramental life and language of the community into which new believers are gradually incorporated. Ultimately, remembrance exhausts language. We lapse into the silence of God's mysterious presence within our communal lives. Our remembrance of God's *mysterion* then becomes the source for breaking silence in acts of praise, prayer, witness, preaching, and song. From this silence, this *mysterion*, all holy human words are drawn.

"Anima Quaerens Verbum"*

"Mind your tongue," Mother said.
God knows I try.
It works a will of its own,
making a way under barbed wire,
over the posted *NO* zones.

Once I dreamt I dressed it right,
sent it off, proper,
to finishing school.
It showed up at dawn,
barefoot and pregnant again.

You should see what follows it home.
It twists into curio corners.
It may market a flea,
retrieve a retro,
auction a Grandma Moses,

It's always a matter of taste.
I am what I eat.
Mouton Cadet. Fry bread and beans.
Crepes flambe and collard greens.
I bless what it senses,
keen to the spices of life.

It consumes the rough skin of wild texts,
savors sharp insight, sweet seeds.
But it hungers for the word
forged from honey, fired like steel,
whose double edge mutes all,
save the single sound:
Holy   Holy   Holy.

I always mind my own tongue.[1]

---

* The soul in search of the word.

F O U R

PRIMITIVE CHRISTIANITY

Primitive:

1. Of or belonging to the first age, period, or stage;

2. Having the quality or style of that which is early or ancient. Also, simple, rude, or rough . . . old-fashioned (with implication of either commendation or the reverse);

3. Original as opposed to derivative; primary as opposed to secondary;

4. *Mathematics:* Applied to a line or figure from which some construction or reckoning begins.[2]

Warning: You have been exposed to a primitive woman's mind. This collection of assorted bits and pieces of traditional liturgical material has been kept on hand on the chance it might someday prove useful. I have arranged some of the pieces into a structured whole, and left others to the side. Three of the standard categories of worship have been addressed: eucharist, baptism, teaching and preaching the Word. In self-defense against the critique that this bricolage approach involves devious means, I admit that I leave a few inductive wires lying about.[3] This "bits and pieces" liturgical approach lacks the formal manners of a theology of worship. The desire to make transformational contact between self and Other (God, world, community) can lead to hasty conclusions and primitive connections. Nevertheless, this desire to overcome the separation we suffer is a worthy desire. *Imago Dei* humans are empowered by the meaning that comes from contact with all that is holy, worthy, and human. *Bricolage* depends on this direct contact, taking meaning "with the musing of a mind, one with her body."[4]

The question that haunts a bricoleur is not one of method. The challenge is "Does it work?" I have taken meaning, but have I given meaning? I have assembled a language of praise, *weorthscipe*, but is it a private language? Ecstatic utterance has often served to articulate the unheard language of women's hearts. What I have labored over, however, is discerning voices, not speaking in tongues.

In liturgics, the study of worship, we evaluate the forms used in order to discern their function. One woman's private prayer may offer to many women a common language of experience. On the other hand, caution needs to be exercised when claims to the "right way to worship" are made. In our eagerness to claim the authority of the public spheres of pulpit, table, and publication, we may trash a tradition, ignore a hand signal, invalidate voices risking speech.

The very title of this bricolage book is tricky and primitive. *Women?* Too essentialist, too arrogantly inclusive or exclusive. Worship? Too mundane. *Worshiping Women?* Caution. Dangerous connections. The *weorthship* of women creates suspicions that the ambiguity of title contains a not-so-hidden agenda: women's worship is the worshiping of women. We are conceived in the image of God. Are we not worthy of respect, as are all

who are created *imago Dei?* Why has the hallowing of
our experience been forbidden or ignored by tradition?
Where is the humor in the old saying, "All have sinned
and fallen short of the glory of God, but some are
shorter than others"? Why should a community fear the
rising status of women's ministry? When an *imago Dei*
woman straightens her spine through the work of the
Spirit, her full stature is a witness to God's holy design.
The promised dream of a new heaven and earth may
come closer to a waking reality.

Can the interplay of the multiple meanings of *Worshiping Women* serve as a call across the fence to my
unknown neighbor, my unclaimed sister? Does this
invitation to explore the holy-human landscape of worship at a primary level appear too elementary? What if
we begin with childhood's hospitality? Do I risk a backlash from the grown-up guardians of language?

> O playmate,
> come play today with me.
> Climb up my apple tree.
> Play with my dollies three.
> Climb in my rainbarrel.
> Slide down my cellar door,
> and we'll be jolly friends forever more.[5]

What are the means by which women can declare
social location without surrendering relationship? How
do I communicate my own re-location, a move from a
matriarchal household where King James was spoken,
to a seminary setting where faculty sisters work in
mother tongues which are diverse, disciplined, and
spirited? Have the midwives of the church who taught
me to say "Jesus" been properly valued for their faith
and resistance? Will the fierce and whimsical circle of

women who have made an exodus from the established church continue to welcome those who maintain Christian credentials?

I mourn the loss of worthy women from a faith community that does not want to admit the loss. Often I appear old-fashioned (i.e., primitive) in my loyalty to a particular religious tradition and its living members. I ask myself repeatedly why I presume a female shape for the construction called church? It seems simply a recognition of the obvious: women were my teachers of the holy text and context. At my most primitive level of perception, reality is constructed female and churched. Women were the caregivers and consensus makers, movers and shakers. Men preached, decreed, but church was where women's language took on flesh.

I have two separate households surrounded by the word "church." In the summer it meant a West Virginia mountain chapel with a shrinking family circle and a dying economy. The paid preacher came once a month, but old Mrs. Hess was the mother of many conversions. She'd scan the handful who had gathered in the pews and the few who hovered by the door. When the Spirit nodded, she would take her place beside you. No social rules ever got in her way. Children and sin-spitting old men experienced her disarming and disconcerting power.

Our winter household of faith was first organized in our living room as a mission in the Arizona desert, moved to a turkey shed, and is now a United Methodist congregation of more than nine hundred members. I have puzzled over the difference in these households and arrived at one similarity: the dying of one and the birth of another made them female structures where women's social and spiritual creativity was nurtured, not spayed. I know and expect to learn more about the painful scarring being inflicted on the intimate lives of *imago Dei* women and men in the name of Christ. I inspect my own body of evidence, yet church was for me enough of an alma mater, a nurturing mother. I still can conceive of and participate in the work of *weorthscipe* reformation.

Creativity can survive within the interstices of the most formal of religious structures. But the distinction between creative and chaotic is usually made by those who remain uncontaminated by either process. This judgment made from a power position exterior to a woman's religious process, renders the holy-human herself of a woman suspect. Vested authority tends to deny validity to experience that appears *too* ontological, too primitive, still under construction.

Our lives, however, require daily composition: discovery and disappointment, recovery and resistance. Enforced social marginality produces rituals of re-formation, which thrive on imagination, interdependence, and are open to the future in life-giving ways. Worship, with its work of praise, is a primitive human response that sustains human life in the present.

> There is a wealth of other social benefits which can come from good praise too: the joy that can overflow mutually, confidence for new ventures and relationships, recognition of the need to face the devastating, joyless consequences of sin and evil, enrichment of culture and personal expression through powerful language, music and gesture, achievement of a common framework for thinking, feeling, imagining and acting, and even an understanding of group dynamics.[6]

A common framework for thinking about women's worship is being constructed from recent scholarship such as Mary Collins' "Principles of Feminist Liturgy" in *Women at Worship: Interpretations of North American Diversity.*[7] Using a short list of critical principles in the discussion of women's patterns of worship provides a working grammar for *godsippe,* yet encourages the integrity of our diversity. Within this framework, *bricolage* appears as genuine and primitive; a method, not madness. To repeat the definition from the opening *prae-texere:*

> It uses a limited, heterogeneous repertoire of inherited bits and pieces. It makes do with whatever is at hand, with a set of tools and materials which is always finite and is also heterogeneous because what it contains bears no relation to the current project, or indeed to any particular project, but is the contingent result of all the occasions there have been to renew or enrich the stock or to maintain it with the remains of previous constructions or destructions.[8]

This chapter's primitive collection has been gathered from my own backyard. My primal memory is a child sitting perfectly still in a little red wagon and imagining everything the family needs to survive a trip to an unnamed destination. My sibling role is "Sister's Sick." My three sisters are instructed to romp around me, careful not to tempt me into active participation.

Exploration is the name of every game. My task is to imagine the necessities we would need: barrels of water, strings for kites and fishing, cloth, candy, dictionaries in every known language, and so forth. I observe the patterns and revise the lists. Sometimes I am consulted for descriptive details of where we are now, but my primary assignment is to imaginatively prepare for the possible worlds we are going to meet. I call this "Wagon

Train." Perhaps some postmodern children play "Star Trek," boldly going where no one has gone before. *Play* seems to be a perfectly primitive way to prepare for a re-formation of worship. A brief summary of play in Victor Turner's article,"Body, Brain and Culture," describes its potential.

> Because of its ability to subvert social structure and overturn customary idea, play can liberate all our definitions of reality. Moreover, since play deals with the *whole gamut* of human experience—both *present* and *historical* (i.e., stored in culture)—it can assume a role in the social construction of reality similar to that played by genetic mutation and variation in organic evolution.[9]

With bricolage and this principle of play in place, let us explore other primitive applications of principles of Christian worship, each one a primitive line or figure from which some construction or reckoning begins. This is a working list, designed to be re-formed whenever a reformation is necessary.

First is last and many is the rule.

(Primitive Christianity and postmodern worship are pluriform in doctrine and practice.)

Paul F. Bradshaw heads a "decalogue of proposed interpretative principles" in *The Search for the Origins of Christian Worship* with a principle that ties a knot in the timeline of liturgical evolution. "What is most common is not necessarily most ancient, and what is least common is not necessarily least ancient."[10] It is delightful for practitioners of primitive Christian worship to discover that simple-to-complex evolution is not a working theory in liturgy (or in form criticism). In addition, the argument of liturgical uniformity for the sake of doctrinal purity should not be applied to the worship patterns of the postmodern church. Liturgy has a long and honest history of being messy and very particular. Our desire to return to a well-ordered golden age will result in a bumpy ride. Primitive Christianity's forms of prayer, praise, and eucharist are diverse, to state it mildly. As Paul Bradshaw observes, "First-century Jewish liturgy, from which Christian worship took its departure, was not nearly so fixed or uniform as was once supposed, and . . . New Testament Christianity was itself essentially pluriform in doctrine and practice."[11]

Primitive Christianity is not ancestor worship.

(Weorthscipe worship authorizes holy-human worth through organic relationships.)

Power and authority are involved in every act of liturgy. To esteem another is an act that creates a position of value for that other. *Weorthscipe* is grounded in the relationships that sustain our lives as worthy. The worship forms we value have a lively, growing nature. They are relational, but they are not to be arbitrarily imposed or universally inherited. Authority with, *not over*, is the critical principle, and it is not restricted to women-only experiences of corporate worship. As Ronald Grimes writes,

> The feminist critique and environmental crisis requires of us men who hold various kinds of ritual authority that we drop our preoccupation with ritual *authorization* so that we have the energy to follow the leads of others who know more than we about ritual *generation.*

The former is typical of the posture of liturgical erectitude; the later, of liturgical supinity. The difference between the two emphases is that the authority question . . . starts at the top (the head) rather than the bottom (the roots). . . . Ritual has (or ought to have) authority only insofar as it is rooted in, generated by, and answerable to its infrastructures—bodily, cultural, ecological, spiritual.[12]

Love to tell the story.

(The relationship between scripture and worship is formed by a narrative which is chosen by the community for its own self-telling.)

Delores Williams's essay "Rituals of Resistance in Womanist Worship" in *Women at Worship* provides another necessity on my primitive list.[13] A community's relationship to scripture and its authority-claim on the patterning of worship is critical for women's worthyship. Delores Williams lines out the oral tradition of the Bible, which constantly reconstructs holy text from human context.

> First, early Christian origins for the black community were in the early slave period of African-American history. That was when they began fashioning a worldview out of the biblical images and stories *they selected* as appropriate to their life situation—the biblical material that spoke the good news on male and female terms. That is when and how their testimonies, songs, and narratives say they met Jesus.[14]

The community's acknowledgment and inclusion of a holy text beyond the printed text is a shared heritage in Appalachian worship. Testimonies of the saints with their patterned language of suffering and the advent of deliverance belong to the unwritten order of worship. Like the African American experience, this oral tradition sustained a community when few of its members could read or write. Its continuing worth is the way it can liberate a congregation from pulpit domination or the restrictive use of scripture. This is a worship principle which in practice hallows a marginalized community's experience, and sustains the memory of God's particular grace in this particular place.

Perception, then conception.

(The human body, that is, a woman's body, is understood to be imago Dei; *worship enables embodied revelation, not able-bodied domination.)*

Weorthscipe worship begins by making sense with the senses. Embodied knowing is to be celebrated, not dismissed as invalid. Incarnation is taken seriously, and the anti-body attitude which flourishes in word-driven, pew-tethered congregations is declared heretical. Diann L. Neu describes this in a liturgy for Pentecost:

> As a liturgy, "Women of Fire" expressed embodied knowledge through kinesthetic auditory, and visual pathways. This made it possible and more comfortable for women with disabilities to participate and provided an arena for everyone to experience the divine in her own embodied way. We emphasized embodied action in the language of space, gesture, sound, color, and nature.[15]

Inclusivity of body means all bodies, not just able bodies. Recent writings by Valerie C. Jones Stiteler and Christine Smith deconstruct the image of holy body = perfectly whole body.[16] Key concepts of God and the human community cannot be communicated without the perceptions of all the embodied community of Christ.

Ask and it shall be given.

(Primary research in women's liturgy acknowledges the oral tradition, that is, communication and communion.)

In this time of migration (geographic, cultural, denominational, linguistic), a pattern of worship should acknowledge its place of origin. Women's experience is that place for many theologians today, perhaps the only norm which is agreed on.[17] But how do we come into contact with "experience"? What means do we have of measuring women's ways of knowing, praising, transforming the world? What does your sister *mean* when she recites the Lord's Prayer? If standard forms of worship are followed in a congregation of men and women, can a woman's experience be discerned?

Twenty-seven years ago, Nelle Morton, teacher of an entire generation of feminists, offered a course at Drew titled, "Women, Language, and God." It marked the beginning of many conversations still being held over coffee, rice wine, across pews and porches, blackboards or babies. This communication-communion "is the contingent result of all the occasions there have been to renew or enrich the stock or to maintain it with the remains of previous constructions or destructions."[18]

Research such as Joanna Gillespie's work, "Gender and Generations in Congregations" opens the experience of "the woman in the pew," revealing both potential and present sources of church re-formation.[19] Mary Catherine Bateson's presentation of five women whom

125

she esteems in *Composing a Life* is another model for discerning women's experience.[20] Some of the silence of history is broken when older narratives are reclaimed, such as *Six Women's Slave Narratives,* in the Schomburg Library of Nineteenth-Century Black Women Writers.[21]

Some of the observations of *Worshiping Women* come from oral interviews given by eighty-four women who participate in the worship life of thirteen differing worship traditions. Interviewing was a rough, primitive process compared with the in-depth research techniques of *Women's Ways of Knowing: The Development of Self, Voice, and Mind.* Nevertheless, the design prompted several pastors to utilize the interviews in order to surface lay women's experiences for congregational planning. The interview questions initiated lively conversation and stirred up a commual "inter-viewing" among the women of the congregation.

- What images come to mind when you hear the expression "worshiping women"?
- Share/draw the kind of space that helps you worship.
    - a. Is it associated with persons?
    - b. How does color/texture/smell/sound/feelings of safety influence you?
    - c. What position of your body do you associate with worship?
- Are there events in your life you wish you could celebrate, or mourn, but there is no form or opportunity for it?
- What parts of a regular worship service would you be comfortable leading? least comfortable?
- What makes a meal holy? Are there particular foods which you find comforting or you associate with being loved?

Commonplace grace.

(Worship is, in its essence, inseparable from the limiting and enriching contexts of body, feeling, relationship, community, history, and the nitty-gritty of life.)

The assumption of commonplace grace and holy ordinariness is the primitive basis for worthy worship. This stated principle is often violated by the practice of permanently "altaring" only certain objects, times, spaces, persons. Practitioners of primitive Christian worship need a common touch so that the tangible evangelism of the sacraments and the sacramental nature of life itself can be grasped. As Judith Plaskow reminds us:

> The self is essentially relational, inseparable from the limiting and enriching contexts of body, feeling, relationship, community, history and the web of life. The notion of the relational self can be correlated with the immanental turn in feminist views of the sacred: in both cases connection to that which is finite, changing and limited is affirmed.[22]

Re-formation is the rite process.

(The process of re-formation involves "rending and renewing"[23] the basic constructs of faith communities. Central to this re-formation is the work of worship.)

Sarah Cunningham invokes this principle in her ecumenical text, which presents the dream of the forming and re-forming of the community of *imago Christi*. When worship enables the practice of this principle, sanctuary is created, the site of human emancipation. Her list of hopes is a litany which re-constructs reality:

There will come a day when:
Each will see the other as created in God's image.
Each will honor the other's gifts and find a way of benefiting from all those gifts.
Some will preach and bear children as well.
Some will prophesy and nurture children as well.
Some will test the spirits.
Some will prepare meals and serve them, as if they were serving the supper of communion . . .
Some will sit on the courts; some in the legislative halls of the nation.
Some will raise our consciousness about the state of the world and our responsibility for righting wrongs.[24]

This is the re-forming dream, which can become a Reforming tradition. We will know as we are known, hold as we are held. Nothing of value will be lost. Everything worth loving is remembered. Through bitter randomness and blessed chaos, God's goodwill is being done. When the day comes that we are worthily received by our alma maters, our fostering-nurturing institutions, God will be glorified. Our chief end in life and worship is to glorify God, or in Elizabeth A. Johnson's words,

> Because God is the creator, redeemer, lover of the world, God's own honor is at stake in human happiness. Wherever human beings are violated, diminished, or have their life drained away, God's glory is dimmed and dishonored. Whenever human beings are quickened to fuller and richer life, God's glory is enhanced.[25]

"What is it that a woman really wants?" (Freud)

(Joy is a holy woman's rite.)
"Glory" is a word now used primarily in human-to-holy relationships. Like the word "praise" it no longer

communicates human social relationships to the same depth of meaning. Frank Henderson's study of medieval prayer books offers a *remembrance* that can deepen our patterns of worship.[26] The *Gloria patri* and the *Magnificat* were common prayers used in England in 1400, but "joy," not "glory," was the human re-sponse offered to God. What difference would it make, Henderson wonders, if "we might give joy or wish joy to God"?

The re-formation of God's people involves a re-formation of our language of worship. Praise, respect, esteem, giving worth to one who is worthy are needed meanings of the word *worship* which were once present in medieval English. Those who practice *bricolage* can use this inherited bit of tradition in order to enliven the holy-human word and action of *worship*.

MAGNIFICAT

My soule worschipeth the lord.
My soul worships the Lord.

And my goost made joye in god: myn helthe.
And my ghost made joy in God, mine health.

For he lokede the mekeness of his handmayde:
For he looked the meekness of his handmaid

lo ther fore alle generations schulle seye y am blessed.
lo therefore all generations shall say I am blessed.

For he that is migty hath do grete thynges to me:
For he that is mighty hath do great things to me

and his name is holy.
and his name is holy.

And his mercy is fro kynrede in to kynredes:
And his mercy is from kindred into kindred

129

to hem that beeth dredynge hym.
to them that be dreading him.

He dyde migt in his arm.
He did might in his arm

he scaterede proude men with thougt of his herte.
he scattered proud men with thought of his heart.

He putte down migti men of the sete;
He put down mighty men off the seat

and heyede meke.
and high-ed the meek.

Hongri men he fylde with goodes:
Hungry men he filled with goods

and riche he lefte empty.
and rich he left empty.

He took up isrl his chyld:
He took up Israel his child

thenkynge on his mercy.
thinking on his mercy.

As hee hadde spoken to oure fadres abraham:
As he had spoken to our father Abraham

and to his seede for euere.
and to his seed for ever.[27]

   This ancient song of praise has generated countless
forms and principles of worship. The physical image
of Mary is allowed out of the attics of Protestant
women only at Christmas, but this powerful invocation of one woman's central place in the work of righting the world is accessible whenever needed. This
Magnificat articulates a standard of experience; it gives
permission to that *joy* which is the outcome of holy-
human women's worship.

Praise actualizes the true relationship between people as well as with God, and it is no accident that in the symbols of heavenly bliss the leading pictures are of feasting and praising. . . . Those also give the clue to one of the most basic things of all about the experience of praise: it is about pleasure. Christianity has been understandably reticent about the joy, bliss, delight and sheer pleasure at its heart. But it is also, simply because its God is the God of joy. Christian hedonism is the holy intoxication of pleasing and being pleased by God, and that sums up the experience of true praise.[28]

Pleasing and being pleased by God and one another is the sum experience of worthy worship. The tension, however, between that sentence and the painful reality of many women's lives produces a ferment that will not be contained. Lament, anger, struggle, and joy are all within the range of holy women's language of praise. The Spirit's fermenting may be sobering, but not forever. New wine is being made; grapes of wrath are being pressed. If old wineskins refuse these new measures and praise, then the *weorthscipe* of *imago Christi* women and men will spill out into the world; a primitive Pentecost will happen all over again.

* * * * *

What does *weorthscipe* require? Righteousness, then rite-ness. *(Fear of doing the wrong thing in a public rite is a primitive impulse that can help or harm worship leaders. When a woman crosses the leadership line between the private sphere of prayer and the public space of institutional worship, there is the added weight of appearing "out of place." A narrative of* weorthscipe *with its triple meanings, can help her to re-form that fear, and release her gifts of ministry.)*

Mothers and Alma Maters

My destination is seminary. My point of departure is the Navajo Reservation in Rough Rock, Arizona. Rough Rock School is the first Navajo school to separate from the Bureau of Indian Affairs, choosing self-government. All those pretty books with fences and sidewalks, elephants and electric mixers, fathers with important papers and mothers who went shopping are discarded. If language is life, this was a matter of life and death. Teachers are hired to make the life of "The People" come to life in texts that honor their context.

I spent several years generating language games, plays, and stories that could connect "The People" to English without severing their own source of language-life. It is an immersion in a culture with sacred language and rituals that bestow life-cycle strength. It is not a Christian culture, but it possesses immense vitality and creativity.

A young girl is absent one morning, and when I ask after her, I am answered with a gesture. "Up the mountain" the children signal with a tip of the head. "Up the mountain" means her time of womanness has come. "Up the mountain" means a young girl is the center of loving and sophisticated rituals being offered by her extended family and clan. "Up the mountain" she will be assured of her "worth" as a woman to her religious community, her family, and herself. When she comes down from the mountain, her face, like Moses', will be altered. A girl goes up the mountain. A woman who knows she is worthy comes down.

By searching for ways to "tell" the sacred stories of this world, a hunger for the sound of my own world and its Word is resurrected. Are there not places in my own culture that are suffering from a disconnection between language and life? Are there not rituals drawn from Scripture that bestow the blessing and the sense of womanness and worth in my own world? The tangible memories of my own cloud of witnesses assure me that the future offers rights and rites to women who are *imago Christi.*

I decide to take the matter of theological application seriously. I set out to apply a variety of theological schools to my chosen life, a kind of literal skin test of sensitivity. I begin going west to California's collection of religious institutions. Having reached the Pacific, I then reverse direction, and travel toward the other ocean. The journey is a journey in search of a home. Where do worshiping women belong? What kind of institutional shape, what form of theological process offers hospitality to *weorthscipe* women?

The one notable detour of process occurs as I sit filling out an application form in the student union at Southern Methodist University. Two neatly tied young men introduce themselves at my booth. I clear the papers to make room for our coffee, an act of hospitality that goes unrewarded. What follows is an hour-long wrangle about Scripture and tradition and the God-given limits of women and worship. I develop a certain resistance to these male voices of authority pronouncing me unworthy of Christ's call.

(Once I heard an assurance of "worthy" spoken by the pastor of my childhood. He heard the Spirit moving in my life, and this single act of hearing was sufficient to withstand the finger-in-ear behavior of the other patriarchs I would encounter.

Twenty years passed between his first blessing and the second. I came as the guest preacher prior to his

departure from a well-served church. Greetings at the
door were charged with the unspoken "Goodbye." He
wore hearing aids, one for each ear. His hearing loss
was irreversible and would someday be total. He prepared for the future by learning to lip-read. When he
knelt, face-to-face with a four-year-old girl, to catch
what she wanted him to know, I remembered how he
had esteemed me with the same careful attention. Nelle
Morton is right. We can hear each other into life.[29] We
esteem another's being by being present for them, an
act of *weorthscipe*.)

My would-be converters depart disappointed. I
return to the journey, alerted to the reality that perfect
strangers would invoke a vengeful God to chastise me
publicly for my vocation. I leave the interrupted application on the table. Years later I learn that the two men
are on a mission for God, sponsored by a rival seminary
in Dallas. It is standard practice to proselytize (or its
reverse) in the heart of the enemy's camp.

I reach my family's holy land, a farm in Palestine,
West Virginia, to make peace with my origins. The primal work of mothers and daughters is that of making
distinctions, not separations. Pre-oedipal connections
are the human given for all those "born of a woman."
The social arrangements of that biological force engage
the energies of women and their mothers for a lifetime.
Our matrixed family makes that a religious quest. I was
nearly twenty before I could verbalize a long-held suspicion that God is a reality capable of independence
from my mother. To my knowledge, my mother has
never confirmed this probability.

The choice of a religious alma mater is obviously a
major event for such a mothered daughter. I fix on the
most powerful of male institutions, the name of all

names, "Harvard." I have engendered enough of my Scot father's fixed determination that I believe I can attempt the translation into male space. Curiosity and desire keep me circling the walls of this castle. My mother's request to see this matriarch of alma maters decides the matter. We set out with the arrogance of cats to visit the Queen.

I park the pickup and call a cab so that our arrival can be anonymous. My mother proceeds to engage the driver in the intimate details of our quest. We arrive at the Yard. I pay the fare, and just as we exit, he delivers a prophecy as if he'd been consulted. "Lady, don't go to Harvard. God is dead at Harvard."

Mother is staggered by the revelation. I tell her to keep walking; he is a cab driver, not a theologian. I deposit her on the bench at the entrance, tell her firmly to sit and wait for my return. I can see the troubling signs of an inspiration coming on. I do not require her spirited maternal intervention. In fact, it appears as if we have tracked something in on our feet that does not belong. The stony patina of this Queen of the sciences appears impervious to charismatic appeal.

I climb the stairs to what I hope will be a normal encounter with an admissions officer. It is formal, cautious on both parts. I depart after a reasonable length of time, determined to apply. The choice of one's alma mater is critical for daughters. One hopes for protection and a merging of identity with the most powerful source of social being. Unlike pre-oedipal connections, however, the merging of institutional and individual female identity is not natural. A successful Harvard application would remove any suspicions about my own marginal maternal origins.

My mother is not where I left her. After several forays

into stony doorways, I sit and wait for her on the bench. She emerges from a basement stairwell, lugging a box of discounted textbooks she has purchased with her social security check. I grumble, but am touched, and we set off in search of a cab.

My plan is to complete the application that night and deliver it before we journey on toward Duke, the Harvard of the South. By the time we reach the highway, the plan changes. I never apply.

(What happens between the bench and the books is an example of a woman's relationship to institutions that have historically marginalized women. Some women simply ignore boundaries, drawing on an internalized sense of blessing. They turn their marginalized position into a "righteous remnant" identity. They speak with the inner authority of Spirit, suspicious of the vested authorities who dismiss their voiced experience as "devious means." The gift of such marginality is that these women can walk away from "established lines of communication. But the lingering pain comes from the haunting suspicion of unworthiness, a rejection by the alma maters of authority.)

Mother claims that she waited "for the longest time," then decided I needed her help. If I want to storm these barricades, she will lead the advance. "Women when they are old enough to have done with the business of being women and can let loose their strength, must be the most powerful creatures in the world."[30] She found the first office empty, made her way into the second and sat down.

That office happens to belong to the Dean of the Seminary, Krister Stendahl. His secretary had momentarily stepped out, and my mother steps in, making herself at home. Her later account of their conversation is decidedly one-sided, but Harvard's Dean emerges as a trifle unbending, eager to restore the order of his day, yet considerate enough to recommend a certain professor whose research might be of interest. He declines my mother's offer of her tithe toward the cost of my tuition, and escorts her out.

Sent back to the bench, my mother again waits for what she considers a reasonable time, then goes in search of the named professor. A mother has certain prerogatives. She intends to use them on my behalf. If this was to be my alma mater, she wants to have a mother-to-mother talk.

She tracks the professor to a floor that is divided between library stacks and doorways. She picks one she later swears is unmarked and swings it open. The occupant of the room is startled into immobility, so is my mother. She has intruded on a man and his urinal. After a silence, he manages a modicum of speech. "May I help you?" he asks. "Oh yes!" Mother replies, grateful for any exit. "I'm looking for Professor _____."

"If you give me a moment, I'll meet you in my office," is his reply, which causes me to swerve out of traffic, turn off the engine, and lean my head against the steering wheel. My camouflage of proper, ordered language was gone. Our family matrix of creativity and chaos has been exposed, shamed. I have no hope of learning how to do the rite thing at Harvard.

What is it that requires law, order, governance, commands? Is this Word of body and earth, of connection and transformation, of difference and specificity, not the precondition for the Word of the order? Underneath the order, what is the substance that so fearfully stands in need of order, what is the frontier that must have boundaries, the limitless chasm that must be rimmed? Is there in this Word of body and earth, of creation and transformation, a limitless possibility that joins with the limitless possibility that is repressed in woman's marginality? If the Word of the order must make itself so strong and so powerful, what power is it resisting, except that of this other Word, hidden, repressed, expelled?[31]

My final year at my self-selected seminary is hectic and heuristic. I serve as coordinator of Religion and Art for Duke University Chapel. I am recruited by Helen Crotwell, minister to the university, and given the necessary sanctuary I need for the balancing of theological chaos and creation. It is Helen who summons me to lunch with the visiting preacher of the week: Krister Stendahl. I had once confided in her my curious story of why I didn't go to Harvard.

Our group gathers for lunch and I stay to the far corner, passing the salt, and keeping quiet. It is humanly impossible to connect my presence and my mother's memory, but I want to take no chances with such a public figure as the Dean of Harvard. It is with great dismay that I hear Helen begin to describe my work. I should have been blessed by her public affirmation; the effect is just the opposite. I concentrate fiercely on my apple pie. He swivels his tall body to look directly at me. I straighten, smile. I resemble my father most when I smile. Helen adds, "You know, it's a shame you missed her at Harvard. I think her mother applied."

A long, very long silence. I grip my spoon, and volunteer nothing. Finally he nods. "A little woman. Very . . . verbal . . ." Everyone at the table waits for my response.

The most explicit acts of worship are times of active receptivity open to a God who can give in a flash what will take a lifetime to work out, apply and conceptualize. Praise is always overflowing where we have got to in thought and action, as it risks greater and greater receptivity and response, and so it becomes the catalyst of prophetic knowledge of God . . .[32]

The choice is clear: distance myself from the old shame of being the daughter of a woman who broke rules and never did the "rite" thing or . . . or what? I look at this powerful father figure, honored son of Tradition's alma mater. I have a sudden image of my mother, a small woman made smaller from illness and a hunched spine, marching uninvited over his threshold and taking a chair to speak, *ex cathedra*, on my behalf.

What can I do but laugh? Social embarrassment turns into my public delight at God's sense of humor. My mother went to Harvard. Perhaps I should have applied, but it is clear her presence was sufficient for both of us. My mother, I could say, went to Harvard. She, I, we were worthy women, capable of discerning God's goodwill. My deep-seated fear of doing the wrong thing in a public rite is replaced with the dangerous liberty of a woman who wants to worship rightly. I made peace at this table, which had certainly been prepared with all my connections, pre-oedipal, postmodern, and primitive. Joy to God, our Alma mater.

APPENDIX

BRICOLAGE: RE-FORMED PRAISE

This is liturgical bricolage, one gathering of bits and pieces of inherited language for the purpose of repair or invention. The workers of women's worship have struggled over the issues of permanent textual forms. Many worship events are just that, *events,* not texts.[1] If a worship has been "of service" to a community in a particular time, place, and social location, can it be transplanted? And if it can, should it be? Can one "borrow" worship forms from racial, ethnic, and religion traditions other than one's own? Does a simple claim to "woman" give permission for sacramental raiding of another's sacred dress? Can a rainstick from Chile be used ethically as a means of "remembering our baptism and being thankful"?

The questions are critical; the answers worshiping communities give are contradictory.[2] One observation seems to be holding: Christianity is a "borrowing" religion. We have inherited a *bricolage* of worshiping traditions. (The Christmas tree is a commonplace example of Christendom's colonization of sacred objects of native cultures.) The actual presence or a respectful esteeming of the people whose ritual prayer or practice is being "borrowed" is a basic requirement for *weorthyscipe.*

Women have historically practiced "borrowing"; the worship books of national gatherings for lay and clergy women are shared with those who could not attend. But as Mary Collins points out in her essay "Feminist Liturgical Principles," successful ritualizing is more *event* than printed form.

Nevertheless, the publishing trade is reinvesting in texts of women's worship. "By the 1850s, *Harper's Magazine* estimated that four-fifths of the reading public were women—to whom culture had been relegated, along with religion, morality, child care, and other nonprofit activities."[3] Women's prayers, parament designs, music, and liturgical theology texts are now available to local congregations. Each prayer represents a world; each rubric reveals a particular household of God.

This particular collection of liturgical bric-a-brac comes from several households of faith: a beloved congregation in West—by God—Virginia, a Fellowship gathering in Junaluska, a confirmation class in northern New Jersey, and a Holston Conference Ministers' retreat. Each offers its partial witness to the only One who is wholly worthy of worship.

Coming of Age in the Body: a Proclamation of Word

The monologue "Daughter of Jairus" is designed to be read by a girl during Eastertide, following her Confirmation or Affirmation of Faith within her community. She reads the Gospel and then reads or recites her monologue. A hymn, such as Ruth Duck's "Wash, O God, Our Sons and Daughters," would continue the proclamation of the gospel. The sermon should draw the interpretative work together or develop a related commentary on the text. The responsibility of "newly turned" women to read and interpret scripture is an initiation practice of Jewish worship that Christian communities need.

The Daughter of Jairus

(To be read with Luke 8:40-56)
I heard the news today.
Jesus is alive.
For once in my life, I can say,
"Didn't I tell you so?"
I told them he'd come back.
I told them not to cry.
He was only asleep,
not dead and gone forever.
Why are grownups so forgetful?
I remember when the fever came
and burned away my mind.
My father ran from street to street,
hunting for the Nazarene.
The bad-news bringers said I died.
They told Jesus not to bother.
But Jesus didn't listen.
They couldn't tell him so.
He came and stood beside my bed and said,
"She isn't dead. Don't cry. She's just asleep."
He took my hand, and touched my eyes,
and said, "Arise."
I told them so!
I told them not to cry.
He was not dead. He was asleep.
God stood beside his bed,
touched his hand and eyes and said, "Arise."
I really want to see him.
I think he knows,
but I want to say,
"I told them so!"[4]

143

Angels Are Back in Style:
a Liturgy for Angelic Hosts

Angels are back in style,
never mind how
many can dance on the head of a pin.

Mall aisles are cluttered
with fluttering fantasies,
victories of victorian sin.

Fat and sassy.
Slim, serene.
No style is missing,
except the seraphim.

So who could market
raging tongues,
unnerving eyes,
hot coals and tongs?

Yet in the undertone of "Hark, the Herald"
"Holy, Holy" can be heard.
And in the aftertaste of angelfood,
some scorching truth remains.[5]

This service is an exercise of "memory and imagination."[6] It was jointly drawn from the work of a visual artist, Laura Flippen; a musician, Wilma Jensen; a preacher, Peter Weaver; and myself. This sharing of design is a necessary process in the re-formation of worship. Setting the text and context for a worshiping community requires a communal discerning. The frustration of such a corporate undertaking is that only the text remains after the event, a bare-bone reminder of a lively encounter of body and Spirit.

The *memory* work of the liturgy involved angelic hosts drawn from scripture and lullabies. The *imagination* came from our fierce desire to serve as guardian angels for our children and all those who have no protection from "the arrow that flies by day" and "the pestilence that stalks by night." The temptation to escape into nighttime nostalgia with a children's song is crossed by the 91st Psalm. The interweaving acknowledges the suffering of the innocent, but affirms God's nature as an active Presence who resists evil and links God's self-worth to our worth.

ENTRANCE

OPENING VOLUNTARY

"Lord, Let at Last Thine Angels Come" (Richard T. Gore)
"Come Down, O Love Divine" (Henry Ley)
"Flight of Angels" (George Frederick Handel)

*GREETING

Let us sing praise to the Sun of Righteousness,
for it is God who said, "Let light shine out of darkness."
**Christ has shown in our hearts
giving us the light of the knowledge of the glory of God
in the face of one another.**

*THE HYMN OF PRAISE

"Maker, in Whom We Live" DIADEMETA
(verses 2 and 4 unison)

*THE OPENING PRAYER

**O Loving Spirit, your birth place is the human heart.
You did not come trumpeting power.
You did not arrive with a rule and a reason.
You came in the holy child Jesus,
and all our birthings were blessed.
Strengthen us in faith
so that we can risk being childlike in love.
This we ask in the name of the One,
who grew in wisdom and in stature
and in favor with God and creation,
Jesus, our brother. Amen.**

*THE ACT OF PRAISE

The Sanctus

PROCLAMATION

The Prayer of Illumination

The Psalm of the Day
    Psalm 91 with Response

The Scripture Lesson (Daniel 3:19-28)
    These are the words of life.
    Thanks be to God.

The Sermon "Angels Watching Over Me"

RESPONSE

The Choral Anthem
    The Children's Choir

An Affirmation of Angels

The times are uncertain.
Landmarks are gone.
How will you find your way?

They who dwell in the shelter of the most high,
who abide in the shadow of the Almighty,
will say to the Lord,
"Our Refuge, Our Fortress,
Our God in whom we trust."

ALL: (sung)

All day, all night, angels watching over me, my Lord.
All day, all night, angels watching over me.

There is a dis-ease in the land.
There are traps laid for the innocent.
Where is the source of your power?

God will deliver us from the snare of the fowler
and from the deadly pestilence.
The pinions of trust will cover us
and under truth's wings we will find refuge.

ALL: All day, all night, angels watching over me, my
Lord.
All day, all night, angels watching over me.

Some who are called will deny.
Some now alive will grow cold.
All who believe will be tested.

A thousand may fall at our side.
Ten thousand at our right hand,

But it will not come near us.
Because we have made the Lord our refuge,
the most high our habitation,
no evil shall befall us,
no scourge come near our tent.

And when it does,
and when it does,
and you have nothing left within
to save your life?

God will give the angels charge of us
to guard us in all our ways.
On their hands they will bear us up,
lest we dash our foot against a stone.

When you stumble,
when you bruise both heart and head,
when they ask you,
"Where is God?"
what will your answer be then?

[silent prayer]

The Holy One has promised,
"Because they cling to me in love,
I will deliver them.
I will protect them
because they know my name.
I will be with them in trouble.
My honor will be their own."

ALL: All day, all night, angels watching over me, my Lord.
All day, all night, angels watching over me.

*THE CLOSING HYMN

"On Eagle's Wings" ON EAGLE'S WINGS
(sung as refrain after solo verses)

*DISMISSAL WITH BLESSING

May Love bless you and keep you;
make your lives shine like the sun.
May God be gracious to you, and you to others.
Lift up your hearts, open your hands
and angels will keep you in peace, now and forever.
Amen.

* CLOSING VOLUNTARY

"Fugue in E flat," S. 552 (ST. ANNE) (Johann Sebastian
Bach)

(The Opening Prayer, An Affirmation of Angels, and
Blessing are by Heather Murray Elkins.)

A Liturgy of Basins: A Maundy Thursday Essay and Service

With the pure in heart I will wash my hands clean, and
take my place among them at thy altar, Lord, listening
there to the sound of thy praises, telling the story of all
thy wonderful deeds. How well, Lord I love thy house
in its beauty, the place where thy own glory dwells!
Lord, never count this soul for lost with the wicked, this
life among the bloodthirsty; hands ever stained with
guilt, palms ever itching for a bribe! Be it mine to guide
my steps clear of wrong; deliver me in thy mercy. My
feet are set on firm ground; where thy people gather,
Lord, I will join in blessing thy name.

(Ps. 26:6-12, Missale Romanum)

149

A priest stands, facing the altar, preparing for the Holy Meal of the sisters and brothers of Christ. The water is poured and then the towel is used and undergirding this gesture of servanthood, an ancient prayer based on Psalm 26 is prayed. For centuries, men who broke the bread and lifted the cup expressed in this liturgical gesture a commonplace act. Hands are washed. A meal is prepared. A meal is eaten. This act of ritual and practical cleansing may have more to do with human instinct than culture or custom. The Christian practice can trace its source to the ritual life of the Temple as reflected in the words of the psalmist.

A certain touch of irony is present in this liturgical gesture which accompanies the preparation of communion. Jesus refused to equate "clean hands and pure hearts" in the fifteenth chapter of Matthew. "Then the Pharisees and scribes came to Jesus from Jerusalem and said, 'Why do your disciples break the tradition of the elders? For they do not wash their hands before they eat.'" The corrective tension between liturgy and life is essential in keeping a balance at the table. We *sense* a need for ritual cleansing, particularly in relationship to eucharist. Our table manners have an effect on holy dining.

For many churches, this liturgical need has taken the form of *foot* washing, based on the account found in John 13:1-17. Some congregations, such as the Mennonites, have participated in a weekly service. Other traditions, including the papal service in Rome, have located the practice in their Maundy Thursday services.

Within Protestant communities, there are now several alternatives. A service of foot washing is featured in *Handbook of the Christian Year*. In an earlier publication, *Ritual in a New Day* (Abingdon, 1976), Jeanne Audrey

Powers outlines the relationship between this liturgical act and its implication for the ministry of our "Servant-Lord." She describes the reluctance of many liturgists to attempt this embodied prayer-act in congregations where sacramental action is privatized, not communal.

Powers considers the possibility of hand washing as a more efficient equivalent, but dismisses it on two grounds: one, the biblical associations with Pilate (washing hands), and two, the absence of the primary meaning, "the prescribed physical activity."

Rather than dismiss her critique, I want to follow its stream to its source of Word and sign. I had been startled by the first priestly hand washing I'd seen, having been raised in a Word-oriented tradition. The sight of the lavabo immediately stirred in me an image of Pilate. I had to work at dismissing the phrase that came to mind, "washing his hands of the whole affair." The combination of the scriptural imprint and this common expression signaled an image, a *theoria* that had chaotic-creative power.

Several years later, that submerged image surfaced. I was involved with planning a Maundy Thursday service in our church. The worship committee was clear about their desire for a form of ritual cleansing yet refused to consider foot washing. Someone had heard of a service that included a "servant's basin" and hand washing.

As we talked, the image of Pilate intruded, "polluting" the concept of servanthood. This time I did not discard or attempt to displace the ambiguous image of hands-water-Pilate-sin. The image was "named" instead. A "Pilate's basin" was necessary in order to have a "servant's basin." Once this "naming" happened, the work-worship of the group became highly charged.

What would a Pilate's basin look like? What kind of towel? What texture would the experience offer? Contrasts quickly developed. Elegant antiques versus aluminum pitchers, cold water in contrast to warm-scented water, church kitchen dishtowels in contrast to wine-colored towels. The gender difference in service was apparent. The mere mention of kitchen towels led to a wry observation that "do this in memory of me" was easier to do in the sanctuary. Deacon Sypher's passing of the cup and Samantha's "holy right of women" were clear. Nevertheless we sensed that the gospel had just emerged from the birth waters of this liturgy.

By maintaining the integrity of the images which had emerged from everyday language and scripture, a theological problem arose. What could carry a congregation from "washing their hands of the whole affair," to the cold water of discipleship and the rough edges of dishtowels? Forgiveness. Community. A fresh start.

These words led to the wellspring of all ministry: baptism. Only the waters of baptism could wash away our sins of omission, the bright stains of complicity with oppressive powers. Only an act of "remembering" and "giving thanks" could purify us to the place where we could risk getting our hands dirty for others.

Three basins and a trinity of affirmations of faith were the means of this journey from Pilate to the towel. *Pilate's Basin:* "Remember, you cannot wash your sins away." The *Basin of Baptism:* "Remember your baptism and be thankful." The *Servant's Basin* and the final words before the Table: "Do this in memory of me."

The service was designed for Maundy Thursday, and the hand washing took place within the communion service. A brief explanation was given before the service began. The passage from John 13 was the text for the sermon. The eucharistic prayers were offered, and the congregation was invited to the table by way of the basins.

The first year we covered the sound of the movement with music. The second year silence prevailed. Like the sound of water, the words of each basin mixed and mingled: "Remember, you cannot wash your . . . Remember your baptism . . . Do this in memory . . . Remember . . . Remember . . . Remember . . ."

Items and Persons for the Service of Basins

Pilate's Basin
small table placed at rear of nave
1 large pitcher and basin, ceramic
1 lace tablecloth
hand towels, wine-colored or embroidered
   (1 towel—3 persons)
extra pitcher with warm water
container under table for basin water
warm water with bath oil
1 server to pour water
1 server to wipe hands and say, "Remember, you cannot wash your sins away."

Basin of Baptism
small table placed at rear of nave in center aisle
1 large crystal serving bowl
   (Font can be used if movable.)
1 shell for pouring water
1 smaller bowl for catching water from shell
white linen napkins (1 napkin—2 persons)
extra pitcher of water
1 server to use shell

1 server to wipe hands and say, "Remember your baptism and be thankful."

The Servant's Basin
small table placed at rear of nave·
1 large dishpan and metal pitcher
newspaper on the table as "cloth"
dishcloths (1 cloth—3 persons)
extra pitcher
container under table for basin water
1 server to pour
1 server to wipe hands and say, "Do this in memory of me."

Rubrics

The service takes place following the Great Thanksgiving. Pastor signals servers to take their places during a hymn.

Invite congregation to come to communion via the basins.

Pastor should go first.

Move to Pilate's basin, extend hands over basin.

A small amount of water is poured in the hands, then the hands are dried as the words are spoken.

Move to Baptism basin, then Servant's basin.

The pastor takes her place to preside at the Table with the stewards.

Members can remain at the altar railing or return to their seats after receiving the elements.

Replace the basin servers with 3 other pairs who have received communion so that the original servers can proceed through the basins and participate in the Table.

The Prayer after Communion follows. The service concludes with a hymn and the Dismissal with Blessing.

Many Protestant churches do not offer clear channels for public or private confession and absolution. This service appears to offer the means for the corporate body to confess and receive assurance of pardon. It also prompts an awareness of mission, which seems to be drawn out of a new understanding of the ministry of the baptized.

Pastoral insight and creativity is needed for the choice of the servers. The basin of Baptism was reserved for the confirmands. They were offered the voice of discipleship. They were not "just to be seen" in the community of believers. The Servant's Basin gained its deepest nonvocal meaning when those who were the servants of the "servants" stood at its setting of dishpan, cold water, and daily news. The most striking memory comes from the year that Sonny, a member with cerebral palsy, wiped our hands with fierce erratic gestures of love.

The particular narrative of a community can surface in this Service of Basins. Pilate's basin was often an antique washbasin and pitcher with an ancestor story attached. The linen napkins often unfolded the unused memories of long-ago weddings or teas. Luther's vision of "the priesthood of all believers" never failed to surface as I stood at the table and waited. "With the pure in heart I will wash my hands clean, and take my place among them at thy altar, Lord."[7]

Stained Glass and the Gospel: an Example of Tangible Evangelism

Symbols cannot be invented; sometimes they can be invoked. Rich traditions lie jumbled in the church drawer. A bricoleur of liturgy can untangle the pieces and lay them out on a table to see if they prompt new conversations in the community.

I had been invited to design the worship services for a ministers' retreat. I asked for an image that would describe the general mood and mind of this particular gathering. "Broken," was one answer. "Fragmented," was another. "Angry. Hurting" was the third.

The retreat design called for an opening service of preaching and a concluding service of communion. Laura Flippen, a visual artist, was consulted for help in designing a room arrangement that could go from work to worship. There were sharp limitations on the physical space, so we shifted focus to tangible experience, which would be both corporate and personal.

Broken glass. Blood. Stained glass. This was the image that surfaced as I reviewed the bits and pieces of the context of this service. Most of the pastors who would be gathering in this retreat led lives of worship surrounded by stained glass. There was no stained glass in the space we were going to be in. What would it mean to create a piece of stained glass from the broken, hurting pieces of this community's life?

Laura could obtain the pieces of glass from a local artisan. How would we bring the people and the glass together without causing further damage? Boundaries of privacy needed protection; fingers needed protection. "Wrap it," was her answer. Right. Wrap it we did, in fading pages of paperback copies of *The Good News for Modern Man*. Each broken piece, with its own distinctive color and edge, was wrapped in a piece of "good news."

The stained glass was used as a reverse offering, in response to the Word. Those who were willing to "claim a brokenness" were invited to come forward for their sharp-edged good news. The large basket was left beside the door after the service for those who might not want to take a piece in front of others. The single instruction was to keep the piece of glass until the closing communion when there would be an opportunity to offer it up.

Humans need meaning like oxygen. Narratives of gospel and glass started from the moment the glass touched a hand. The public, private, and multiple meanings of this symbol gathered strength with each passing day.

One event among many involved two men, old friends deeply embittered by a rivalry of appointments. They could not talk about the brokenness between them. They met in a hallway the day after the glass had been given. Instead of passing without a word, they stopped, each spontaneously extending to the other the piece he was carrying. It happened once; it happened a hundred times. The tangible evangelism of this symbol created narratives of freedom and forgiveness. Even the no-nonsense Bishop was startled to discover the text for his closing sermon wrapped around his piece of stained glass.

The final form of the glass could not be completed within the timeframe of the conference. Some forms of worship require a long time to gestate, to grow into their proper shape. This particular form was later used in a national conference for the Fellowship of Musicians and Other Artists. The wrapping for the glass came from old hymnals, and the symbolic life of music was added to its power.

The finishing of the Word and glass design came a year after the ministers' retreat. I asked Ashley

Calhoun, a gifted liturgist of the conference, if he would take responsibility for the glass which would be offered up as members of the conference came for communion.

I remember the surprising silence which followed my request. In place of a yes or no answer, I learned of the sudden, tragic loss of his brother, who had been a stained-glass artist. Ashley asked for the pieces. A year later, he had lovingly assembled a cross, framing the sharpness of grief with the fragments of glass. From the jagged edges and brokenness of one community comes an *imago Christi* sign of resurrection for many.

NOTES

Preface

1. Claude Levi-Strauss, *The Savage Mind* (Chicago: University of Chicago Press, 1966), p. 74.

2. Ibid., p. 16.

3. Adrienne Rich, from "Transcendental Etudes," in *The Fact of a Doorframe: Poems Selected and New* (1950-1984) (New York: W. W. Norton, 1984), pp. 268-69.

4. Robert Ranulph Marett, *Faith, Hope, and Charity in Primitive Religion* (New York: Macmillan, 1932), p. 109.

5. Levi-Strauss, *The Savage Mind*, p. 17.

6. Ibid.

7. Ibid.

8. James F. White, *Introduction to Christian Worship* (Nashville: Abingdon, 1980), p. 25.

9. Evelyn Underhill, *Worship* (Harper & Brothers, 1937), p. 3.

10. See Elizabeth A. Johnson's chapter "Women's Interpreted Experience" in *She Who Is* (New York: Crossroad, 1993), for her scholarly reformation of the theological insights conveyed by the terms *imago Dei* and *imago Christi*.

Chapter 1: Women's Water Rites

1. Heather Murray Elkins, "Diamonds Are Forever," © 1993.

2. Elisabeth Schüssler Fiorenza, *Bread Not Stone: The Challenge of Feminist Biblical Interpretation* (Boston: Beacon Press, 1984), pp. 74-75.

3. Marjorie Hewitt Suchocki, *God, Christ, Church: A Practical Guide to Process Theology* (New York: Crossroad, 1989), p. 59.

4. Herman C. Waetjen, *A Reordering of Power: A Socio-Political Reading of Mark's Gospel* (Minneapolis: Fortress Press, 1989).

5. Ibid., pp. 67-71.

6. Anthony Giddens, *Modernity and Self-identity: Self and Society in the Late Modern Age* (Stanford: Stanford University Press, 1991).

7. *Didascalia Apostolorum, XVI*, trans. R. Hugh Conolly (Oxford: Clarendon Press, 1969), pp. 146-47 as cited by James F. White, *Documents of Christian Worship: Descriptive and Interpretive Sources* (Louisville: Westminster/John Knox Press, 1992), p. 156.

8. Ibid.

9. Marjorie Procter-Smith, *In Her Own Rite: Constructing Feminist Liturgical Tradition* (Nashville: Abingdon Press, 1990), p. 53.

10. Ibid.

11. White, *Documents of Christian Worship,* p. 149.

12. Elizabeth A. Clark, *Women in the Early Church, Message of the Fathers of the Church,* ed. Thomas Halton, vol. 13 (Collegeville, Minn.: Liturgical Press, 1983).

13. Ibid., p. 85.

14. *Corpus Scriptorum Ecclesiasticorum Latinorum* 20.215, as cited by Elizabeth A. Clark, *Women in the Early Church,* p. 173.

15. This chapter was being written during "The Re-Imagining Conference," held in Minneapolis, November 1993, to celebrate the Ecumenical Decade—Churches in Solidarity with Women. Mainline denominations continue to register afterquakes to this conference. As of spring '94, the Women's Division of the General Board of Global Ministries has been accused of sponsoring heretical teachings by some leaders in the *Good News* movement. United Methodist bishops are being asked to evaluate the orthodoxy of the conference worship texts and speakers. Staff members of the Presbyterian Church, who participated in the general planning of the event, have been targeted for removal by *The Presbyterian Layman.* Christian women's right to name the divine names of God remains a matter of controversy in the twentieth century.

16. Suchocki, *God, Christ, Church,* p. 59.

17. Ruth C. Duck, *Gender and the Name of God: The Trinitarian Baptismal Formula* (New York: Pilgrim Press, 1991).

18. E. C. Whitaker, *The Baptismal Liturgy* (London: SPCK, 1965), p. 9, as cited in Duck, *Gender and the Name of God,* p. 134.

19. Duck, *Gender and the Name of God,* pp. 185-86. Reprinted by permission of The Pilgrim Press, Cleveland, Ohio, as found in *Gender and the Name of God: The Trinitarian Baptismal Formula,* Ruth C. Duck, copyright 1991.)

20. See Barbara Ehrenreich, Deirdre English, *For Her Own Good: 150 Years of the Experts' Advice to Women* (New York: Anchor Books, Doubleday, 1978), pp. 33-39.

21. Heinrich Kramer and Jacob Sprenger, *Malleus Maleficarum: The Hammer of Witches,* ed. Pennethorne Hughes, Montague Summers (London: Folio Society, 1968), p. 218.

22. Procter-Smith, *In Her Own Rite,* p. 53.

23. Letty M. Russell, *Church in the Round: Feminist Interpretation of the Church* (Louisville: Westminster/John Knox Press, 1993), p. 184.

24. Ibid.

25. Procter-Smith, *In Her Own Rite,* pp. 153-60.

26. Ann Patrick Ware, "The Easter Vigil: A Theological and Liturgical Critique," *Women at Worship: Interpretations of North American Diversity,* ed. Marjorie Procter-Smith and Janet R. Walton (Louisville: Westminster/John Knox Press, 1993), p. 96.

27. Duck, *Gender and the Name of God,* p. 42.

28. *We Belong Together: Churches in Solidarity with Women,* ed. Sarah Cunningham (New York: Friendship Press, 1992), p. 120.

29. See resources such as *Into Action . . . Resources for Participation in the Ecumenical Decade, Churches in Solidarity with Women, 1988-1998.* Order #1522 from the U.S. Office of the Ecumenical Decade for Women, 475 Riverside Drive, Room 915, New York, NY 10115.

30. William Zinsser, ". . . Until Justice Rolls Down Like Waters," *Smithsonian* (Sept. 1991), p. 35.

31. Ibid., p. 36.

32. Ibid.

33. Ibid., p. 38.

34. Ibid., p. 35.

35. K. Almond, unpublished paper, "Mountain Woman at Worship" (1993), p. 10.

Chapter 2: Feasting in a Fasting Age

1. Heather Murray Elkins, "Stirring Women," © 1987, revised 1993.

2. Margaret Miles, *Image as Insight: Visual Understanding in Western Christianity and Secular Culture* (Boston: Beacon Press, 1987).

3. Ibid., p. 150.

4. See Horton Davies' most recent work, *Bread of Life & Cup of Joy: Newer Ecumenical Perspectives on the Eucharist* (Grand Rapids: Wm. B. Eerdmans Publishing Co., 1993), for his succinct history and compelling argument of the term "Eucharist."

5. Letty M. Russell, *Church in the Round: Feminist Interpretation of the Church* (Louisville: Westminster/John Knox Press, 1993), p. 17.

6. Ronald L. Grimes, *Beginnings in Ritual Studies* (Lanham, Md.: University Press of America, 1982), p. 90.

7. Women's Action Coalition, *WAC STATS: The Facts About Women* (New York: New Press, 1993), p. 60.

8. Joanna B. Gillespie, "Gender and Generations in Congregations" *Episcopal Women* (Oxford: Oxford University Press, 1992), pp. 167-68.

9. The term "Market" is drawn from the writings of Barbara Ehrenreich and Deirdre English, *For Her Own Good: 150 Years of the Experts' Advice to Women* (New York: Anchor Books, Doubleday, 1978): "To the economic man, the inanimate things of the market-place—money and the commodities which represent money—are alive and possessed of almost sacred significance. Conversely, things truly alive are, from a strictly 'rational' point of view, worthless except as they impinge of the Market and affect one's economic self-interest," (p. 18).

10. Margaret Poloma, *Varieties of Prayer: A Survey Report/Margaret M. Poloma and George H. Gallup, Jr.* (Philadelphia: Trinity Press International, 1989).

11. Mercy Amba Oduyoye, *Who Will Roll the Stone Away? The Ecumenical Decade of the Churches in Solidarity with Women* (Geneva: WCC Publications, 1990), p. 42.

12. Ibid.

13. *Bread of Tomorrow: Prayers for the Church Year*, ed. Janet Morley, (Maryknoll, N. Y.: Orbis Books, 1992), p. 2.

14. Thirty million Americans cannot afford to purchase enough food to prevent the physical and social damage of hunger. See Nancy Chodorow, *The Reproduction of Mothering: Psychoanalysis and the Society of Gender* (Berkeley and Los Angeles: University of California Press, 1978) for the analysis of our culture's psychosocial structures which place women at the "forefront" of this statistic.

15. See Mary Douglas, *Natural Symbols: Explorations in Cosmology* (New York: Pantheon Books, 1970, 1973), for her richly suggestive work in symbolic behavior and the human body.

16. Letty M. Russell, *Household of Freedom: Authority in Feminist Theology* (Philadelphia: Westminster Press, 1987). See also Rosemary Radford Ruether, *Woman-Church: Theology and Practice of Feminist Liturgical Communities* (San Francisco: Harper & Row, 1985); *Speaking of Faith: Global Perspectives on Women, Religion, and Social Change,* ed. Diana L. Eck and Devaki Jain (Philadelphia: New Society Publishers, 1987).

17. Paul Bradshaw, *The Search for the Origins of Christian Worship: Sources and Methods for the Study of Early Liturgy* (Oxford: Oxford University Press, 1992), p. 72.

18. Bard Thompson, *Liturgies of the Western Church* (Cleveland: Meridian Books, 1961; Philadelphia: Fortress Press, 1980), p. 22.

19. Janet Fishburn, *Confronting the Idolatry of Family: A New Vision for the Household of God* (Nashville: Abingdon Press, 1991).

20. Caroline Walker Bynum, *Holy Feast and Holy Fast: The Religious Significance of Food to Medieval Women* (Berkeley: University of California Press, 1987), illustration #28.

21. Margaret Miles, *Images As Insight: Visual Understanding in Western Christianity and Secular Culture* (Boston: Beacon Press, 1985).

22. The following texts are selected for theological diversity out of a rapidly growing body of literature: Virginia M. M. Fabella and Mercy Oduyoye, eds., *With Passion and Compassion: Third World Women Doing Theology* (Maryknoll, N.Y.: Orbis Books, 1988); Elisabeth Schüssler Fiorenza, *In Memory of Her: A Feminist Theological Reconstruction of Christian Origins* (New York: Crossroad, 1984); Marie Marshall Fortune, *Sexual Violence: The Unmentionable Sin* (New York: Pilgrim Press, 1983); Jacquelyn Grant, *White Women's Christ and Black Women's Jesus: Feminist Christology and Womanist Response* (Atlanta: Scholar's Press, 1989); Marjorie Procter-Smith, "Reorganizing Victimization: The Intersection Between Liturgy and Domestic Violence," *Perkins Journal* 40, no. 4 (October 1987), pp. 17-27.

23. Out of the many names for this sacrament (Liturgy, Holy Communion, Divine Service, the Lord's Supper, the Mass, Word and Table), I have elected to use the term "Eucharist." Its basic definition, "giving thanks," describes a vitality of praise that reforms ordinary life, and turns feeding and being fed into an act of worship.

24. WAC, p. 18.

25. Bynum, *Holy Feast and Holy Fast,* p. 270.

26. Annewies van de Bunt "Milk and Honey in the Theology of Clement of Alexandria," *Fides Sacramenti Sacramentum Fidei: Studies in Honor of Pieter Smulders* (The Netherlands: van Goreum Assen, 1981).

27. Ibid., p. 33.

28. Alla Renée Bozarth, "Bakerwoman God," © 1978 Alla Renée Bozarth, found in *Womanpriest: A Personal Odyssey*, rev. ed., LuraMedia, 1988; in *Stars in Your Bones: Emerging Signposts on Our Spiritual Journeys*, by Alla Bozarth, Julia Barkley, and Terri Hawthorne, North Star Press of St. Cloud, 1990; and in the audiotape, *Water Women: Poems by Alla Renée Bozarth*, distributed by Wisdom House, 1990. All rights reserved by author. For permission write to the Rev. Dr. Alla Renée Bozarth 43222, SE Tapp Rd., Sandy, OR 97055.

29. Mary Louise Bringle, *The God of Thinness: Gluttony and Other Weighty Matters* (Nashville: Abingdon Press, 1992), pp. 30-31.

30. Russell, *Church in the Round*, p. 109.

31. "Prayer of Humble Access," Service of Word and Table IV, *The United Methodist Book of Worship* (Nashville: United Methodist Publishing House, 1992), p. 49.

32. Ada Maria Isasi-Diaz, *En la Lucha, In the Struggle: A Hispanic Women's Liberation Theology* (Minneapolis: Fortress Press, 1993), p. 101.

33. Anthony Giddens, *Modernity and Self-identity: Self and Society in the Last Modern Age* (Stanford: Stanford University Press, 1991), p. 105.

34. Gregor Goethals, *The Electronic Golden Calf: Images, Religion, and the Making of Meaning* (Cambridge: Cowley Publications, 1990).

35. Carolyn G. Heilbrun, *Writing A Woman's Life* (New York: Ballantine Books, 1988), p. 15.

36. Ibid., p. 15.

37. Peggy Reeves Sanday, *Divine Hunger and Cannibal Monsters: Cannibalism as a Cultural System* (Cambridge: Cambridge University Press, forthcoming), as cited by Bynum in *Holy Feast and Holy Fast*, pp. 319-20.

38. Bynum, *Holy Feast and Holy Fast*, p. 295.

39. Marietta Holley, *Samantha Among the Brethren* (New York: Funk & Wagnalls, 1890), pp. 263-67. See *Excerpts from Samantha Among the Brethren*, ed. with intro. by Phyllis Eckardt Tholin (Evanston: Phyllis Tholin Books, 1988).

40. Bynum, *Holy Feast and Holy Fast*, p. 276.

Chapter 3: Gospel Gossip

1. Heather Murray Elkins, "The Quilters," © 1985, revised 1993.

2. Elisabeth Schüssler Fiorenza, *Bread Not Stone: The Challenge of Feminist Biblical Interpretation* (Boston: Beacon Press, 1985), pp. 15-22.

3. Jane Schaberg, "Luke," *The Women's Bible Commentary*, ed. Carol A. Newsom and Sharon H. Ringe (London: SPCK, Louisville: West-minster/John Knox Press, 1992), p. 291.

4. Ibid., p. 280.

5. Ibid., p. 281.

6. Ibid., p. 291.

7. Nancy Woloch, *Women and the American Experience* (New York: Alfred A. Knopf, 1984), p. 121.

8. Ibid.

9. Ibid.

10. The five elected were: Angie F. Newman of Lincoln, Nebraska; Mary C. Nind of Minnesota; Amanda C. Rippey of Severance, Kansas; Lizzie Van Kirk of Oakland, Pennsylvania; and Frances E. Willard of Evanston, Ilinois.

11. James M. Buckley, "What Methodism Owes to Women," *Proceedings*, p. 314.

12. Ibid., p. 317.

13. Woloch, *Women and the American Experience*, p. 171.

14. Twentieth-century women came to voice in response to the needs and opportunities of a nation that was also defining itself. As many religious or ethnic groups moved up in social location, the role and status of the women improved:

Although excluded from business and politics, middle-class women were imbued with a positive sense of their roles and responsibilities as women. Benevolence and reform were not merely the most appealing routes to public life for such women, but the only ones. Within the scope of the female association, they extended the skills they already had, in household management, care for the young, concern for the afflicted. They capitalized on their obligations as bastions of piety and guardians of morals. They also created new roles that were parallel or complementary to those of the men in their families—the minister, the lawyer, tradesman, and entrepreneur. Excluded from official channels of authority, middle-class women created their own. (Woloch, *Women and the American Experience*, p. 168)

15. "Women's Right to Preach the Gospel," repr. in Donald W. Dayton, ed., *Holiness Tracts Defending the Ministry of Women* (New York: Garland, 1985), pp. 21-22.

16. Rebecca Laird, *Ordained Women in the Church of the Nazarene: The First Generation* (Kansas City, Mo.: Nazarene Publishing House, 1993), p. 146.

17. Several key texts in this field are: Robin T. Lakoff, *Language and Woman's Place* (New York: Harper & Row, 1975); Lakoff, *Talking Power: the Politics of Language in Our Lives* (New York: Basic Books, 1990); *Language and Sex: Difference and Dominance*, ed. Barrie Thorne and Nancy Henley (Rowley, Mass.: Newbury House Publishers, 1975).

18. *Amazons, Bluestockings, and Crones: A Feminist Dictionary*, selection, intro., and preface Cheris Kranarae and Paul A. Treichler (London: Pandora Press, 1992), pp. 179-80.

19. Rebecca S. Chopp, *The Power to Speak: Feminism, Language, God* (New York: Crossroad, 1989), p. 47.

20. Carol Norén, *The Woman in the Pulpit* (Nashville: Abingdon Press, 1992), p. 70.

21. Ibid., p. 71.

22. Procter-Smith, *In Her Own Rite*, p. 57.

23. Catherine Bell, *Ritual Theory, Ritual Practice* (New York: Oxford University Press, 1992), p. 94.

24. Jean Wyatt, *Reconstructing Desire: The Role of the Unconscious in Women's Reading and Writing* (Chapel Hill: University of North Carolina Press, 1990).

25. Marge Piercy, "Unlearning to Not Speak," *To Be of Use* (New York: Doubleday, 1978), p. 38.

26. Judith Plaskow and Carol P. Christ, eds., *Weaving the Visions, New Patterns in Feminist Spirituality* (San Francisco: Harper, 1989), p. 173.

27. Mary Field Belenky, et al., *Women's Ways of Knowing: The Development of Self, Voice, and Mind* (New York: Basic Books, 1986), p. 162.

28. Helen Gray Crotwell, ed., *Women and the Word: Sermons* (Philadelphia: Fortress Press, 1978).

29. Piercy, "Unlearning to Not Speak," p. 38.

30. Elisabeth Schüssler Fiorenza, "A Feminist Critical Interpretation for Liberation: Martha and Mary: Luke 10:38-42," *Religion and Intellectual Life* 3 (1986), pp. 21-35.

31. Margaret P. Jones, "History and Faith," *Epworth Review*, vol. 20, no. 2 (May 1993), pp. 101-2.

32. Heather Murray Elkins, "The Dance of Mary and Martha" *Women and the Word* (Nashville: EW Press, 1989).

33. Ibid., p. 6.

34. Heather Murray Elkins, "The Prophetess," *Testimony* (Nashville: EW Press, 1988), p. 11.

35. Carlton R. Young, *Companion to the United Methodist Hymnal* (Nashville: Abingdon Press, 1993), p. 431.

36. Chopp, *Power to Speak*, p. 26.

37. Ruth C. Duck, *Gender and the Name of God: The Trinitarian Baptismal Formula* (New York: Pilgrim Press, 1991), p. 81.

38. Ibid.

39. Elkins, "The Quilters," p. 80. In addition to texts referenced in earlier chapters, see Edith Deem, *Great Women of the Christian Faith* (New York: Harper, 1959); Nancy A. Hardesty, *Great Women of Faith* (Nashville: Abingdon, 1980); *Women of Spirit: Female Leadership in the Jewish and Christian Traditions* (New York: Simon & Schuster, 1979), ed. Rosemary Radford Ruether; Elsie Boulding, *The Underside of History: A View of Women Through Time* (Boulder, Colo.: Westview, 1976); Elsie Gibson, *When the Minister Is a Woman* (Troy, Mo.: Holt, Rinehart & Winston, 1970); Kenneth E. Rowe, *Methodist Women: A Guide to the Literature* (World Methodist Council, Lake Junaluska North Carolina, revised 1991); Paul W. Chilcote, *She Offered Them Christ: The Legacy of Women Preachers in Early Methodism* (Nashville: Abingdon Press, 1993); Barbara Brown Taylor, *The Preaching Life* (Cambridge: Cowley Publications, 1993).

40. St. Irenaeus of Lyons, *Against the Heresies,* trans. and annotated by Dominic J. Unger with further revisions by John J. Dillon, vol. 1, book 1 (Paulist Press, 1992), p. 173.

41. Linda Coleman, "Ritual Creedal Language and the Statement of Faith of the Evangelical Women's Caucus," *Women and Religious Ritual*, ed. Lesley A. Northup (Washington: Pastoral Press, 1993), p. 107.

42. Chopp, *Power to Speak*, pp. 24-25.

43. Ibid., 7 and passim.

44. An example of the risk of hearsay becoming heresy can be found in the evolution of Thomas C. Oden's article "Encountering the Goddess at Church," *Christianity Today* (August 16, 1993), which was reprinted in *Good News: The Bimonthly Magazine for United Methodists* (Nov.-Dec. 1993). His article describes a communion service at Drew Theological School as goddess worship. The Reverend Susan Cady, the preacher and a guest lecturer at Drew Theological School, had stated in a recorded public lecture that her use of "Sophia," the Greek word for wisdom, is parallel to the use of the Greek "Logos," the divine word. In this theological framework, "Sophia" refers to God's wisdom, not a goddess.

Yet Cady's sermon reference to divine Wisdom, Sophia, leads to a charge of goddess worship. Oden exits the chapel at the conclusion of the sermon, prior to the beginning of the communion prayers. His article labels the entire service heretical, and the unnamed "highly visible feminist leader" with her "uncommon fixation on the worship of the goddess Sophia," is described as "an unworthy minister."

In a discussion following the event, Oden acknowledges that he has not heard Cady's public lecture. In addition, the radical disagreement between the world of the hearer and the world of the speaker can be seen in her account of a portion of her sermon and Oden's description of the same material. It is important for the reader to note that Sophia is described here as a controversial *issue*. There was no mention in the sermon of a communion ever being offered in the name of a goddess in this local congregation.

Susan Cady:

> One story (which Dr. Oden attributes erroneously to me) is a story of a colleague who had been hounded from the very beginning of her pastorate by a lay member who kept pushing her on controversial issues over which they disagreed, such as abortion, Sophia, and homosexuality. He was more interested in polarizing the church than working on issues of immediate concern to the congregation. The situation had deteriorated to the point where my colleague was questioning her calling. . . . I celebrated an important turning point in my colleague's struggle, when she became aware at a deeper level of her God-given authority in her ordination. She was able to calmly resist the hounding by one or two troublesome lay members and clearly state to the entire congregation the importance of diversity within United Methodism. She made it clear that diverse opinions on many matters were an important aspect of the denomination, and noted that those who were uncomfortable with living with differences might not only be uncomfortable with her, but with the denomination as well. (from correspondence)

Thomas Oden:

> It was a "victory" story in which a pious United Methodist lay leader and other members were driven out of her church and forced to join another after they challenged her authority to offer the Lord's Supper in the name of the goddess Sophia. She

recounted triumphantly how she had preached on the virtues of doctrinal diversity and invited all members who did not agree with her to look for another church. "Encountering the Goddess at Church," *Good News*, 42.

The printed liturgy of this service of Word and Table had been arranged by me, as Chair of the Chapel committee. I presided with Cady at the Table. Our printed communion service was composed of scripture, the historic words of institution, and prayers from *The United Methodist Hymnal* and *The United Methodist Book of Worship*. I have submitted this service to Hoyt Hickman, former chair of the Section on Worship, and several United Methodist bishops. It is, in their evaluation, orthodox, meeting all sacramental standards of United Methodist worship.

The publication history of this service, however, is a case of hearsay becoming heresy. A *Newscope* account (Oct. 22, 1993), reduces Oden's essay to a brief paragraph. The sermon's concluding quote of Proverbs 9:1-6 becomes "the invitation to come to the Lord's Table in Sophia's name," 2. The preacher is unnamed, but is "an unworthy minister" who has "driven out church members who challenged her authority." An essay by Riley Case, "Wither the Seminaries?" *Good News* (Jan.-Feb. 1994), begins with a listing of examples of "paganism" in seminaries. This service is listed in boldface as: "Drew University, the Theological School: Communion is offered in the name of Sophia, goddess of wisdom," 14.

The Knoxville News-Sentinel (Feb. 5, 1994), announces that this service is an "advent of Sophia worship." The service at Drew and the Ecumenical Decade of Women's Re-Imagining Conference are denounced as examples of seminary "teachings [that] are idolatrous." The illustration of a clergywoman's defense of United Methodist theological diversity becomes: "A feminist preached a joyful sermon describing the flight of traditionalists from her church when she offered the Lord's Supper in the name of the goddess," B-4. Other regional papers carry articles and letters to the editor that denounce "goddess communion," and all forms of "womanist/feminist/lesbian worship," *Good News* (Jan.-Feb. 1994).

In March 1994, a new charge of hearsay/heresy is added by Bishop William R. Cannon, "The Cult of Sophia," *Good News* (Mar.-Apr. 1994). The original account of a seminary service, written by a faculty member who departed prior to communion, is now evidence of a cult.

One such service was conducted in the chapel of the Theology School of Drew University, as a substitute—so we have read in news reports—for Holy Communion. It would appear, therefore, that the present day Sophia cult is prominently promulgated by some pastors of the United Methodist Church (16).

45. Marjorie Procter-Smith, *In Her Own Rite* (Nashville: Abingdon Press, 1990), pp. 59-84.

46. See Elizabeth Achtemeier, *Nature, God, and Pulpit* (Grand Rapids: Wm. B. Eerdmans Publishing Co., 1992). Achtemeier acknowledges that theology must encompass more than human creation, but denies that God is immanently present in creation. From her perspective, the theological risk of a multivalent symbol, such as a globe with a crown of thorns, can be more dangerous to Christian worship than the church's long-held neglect of this relationship. She denounces the loss of precise doctrinal boundaries of immanence, and affirms the sharp separation between God and nature. For Achtemeier, "That God is other from his creation and yet works in creation through his Word and Spirit is the basis of Christian hope" (p. 181).

47. Sallie McFague, *The Body of God: An Ecological Theology* (Minneapolis: Fortress Press, 1993).

48. The text of Julian of Norwich, modernized from *A Revelation of Love*, ed. Marian Blasscoe (Exeter: University of Exeter Press, 1988), chap. 5.

Chapter 4: Primitive Christianity

1. Heather Murray Elkins, "Anima Quaerens Verbum," © 1993.

2. *Oxford English Dictionary* (Oxford: Oxford University Press, 1971), pp. 1365-66.

3. Claude Levi-Strauss, *The Savage Mind* (Chicago: University of Chicago Press, 1966), pp. 16-17.

4. Adrienne Rich, from "Transcendental Etudes," in *The Fact of a Doorframe: Poems Selected and New (1950–1984)* (New York: W. W. Norton & Co., 1984), pp. 268-69.

5. Harry Dacre, "Playmates," 1889. *The Great Song Thesaurus*, ed. Roger Lax and Frederick Smith (New York: Oxford University Press, 1989), p. 349.

6. Daniel W. Hardy and David F. Ford, *Praising and Knowing God* (Philadelphia: Westminster Press, 1985), p. 11.

7. Mary Collins, "Principles of Feminist Liturgy," *Women at Worship: Interpretations of North American Diversity*, ed. Marjorie Procter-Smith and Janet R. Walton (Louisville: Westminster/John Knox Press, 1993), pp. 4-18.

8. Levi-Strauss, *The Savage Mind*, p. 16.

9. Victor Turner, "Body, Brain, and Culture," *Zygon* 18:3 (1983), pp. 221-45 as cited in "What Biogeneticists Are Saying About Ritual," *Liturgy Digest* 1:1 (Spring 1993), p. 65.

10. Paul F. Bradshaw, *The Search for the Origins of Christian Worship: Sources and Methods for the Study of Early Liturgy* (New York, Oxford: Oxford University Press, 1992), p. 63.

11. Ibid.

12. Ronald L. Grimes, "Liturgical Supinity, Liturgical Erectitude: On the Embodiment of Ritual Authority," *Studia Liturgica* 23:1 (1993), p. 67.

13. Delores S. Williams, "Rituals of Resistance in Womanist Worship," *Women at Worship*, pp. 215-23.

14. Ibid., p. 222.

15. Diann L. Neu, "Women-Church Transforming Liturgy," *Women at Worship*, p. 172.

16. Valerie C. Jones Stiteler, "Blessing the Darkness: Toward a Feminist Hermeneutic for Worship Which Is Inclusive of Women with Disabilities" (unpublished paper for the Feminist Liturgy Seminary of the North American Academy of Liturgy, 1991); Christine M. Smith, *Preaching as Weeping, Confession, and Resistance: Radical Responses to Radical Evil* (Louisville: Westminster/John Knox Press, 1993).

17. See Monik Hellwig, *Whose Experience Counts in Theological Reflection?* (Milwaukee, Wis.: Marquette University Press, 1982).

18. Levi-Strauss, *The Savage Mind*, p. 16.

19. Joanna B. Gillespie, "Gender and Generations in Congregations," *Episcopal Women: Gender, Spirituality, and Commitment in an American Mainline Denomination* (Oxford: Oxford University Press, 1992).

20. Mary Catherine Bateson, *Composing a Life: Life as a Work in Progress—the Improvisations of Five Extraordinary Women* (New York: Penguin Group, 1990 [Plume repr.]).

21. *Six Women's Slave Narratives*, ed. Henry Louis Gates, Jr. (New York: Oxford University Press, 1988 [Philadelphia: Collins, Printer, 1863]).

22. Judith Plaskow and Carol P. Christ, eds., *Weaving the Visions, New Patterns in Feminist Spirituality* (San Francisco: Harper, 1989), p. 193.

23. Rebecca S. Chopp, *The Power to Speak: Feminism, Language, God* (New York: Crossroad, 1989), p. 76.

24. *We Belong Together: Churches in Solidarity with Women*, ed. Sarah Cunningham (New York: Friendship Press, 1992), pp. 125-26.

25. Elizabeth A. Johnson, *She Who Is: The Mystery of God in Feminist Theological Discourse* (New York: Crossroad, 1993), p. 14.

26. Frank Henderson, "Familiar Prayers in Medieval English," *National Bulletin on Liturgy*, vol. 26, no. 133 (Summer 1993), p. 98.

27. *The Prymer or Prayer-Book of the Lay People in the Middle Ages in English Dating About 1400 A.D.*, Part I: Text, ed. Henry Littlehales (London: Longmans, Green, 1891), pp. 17, 45.

28. Daniel W. Hardy and David F. Ford, *Praising and Knowing God* (Philadelphia: Westminster Press, 1985), p. 11.

29. Nelle Morton, *The Journey Is Home* (Boston: Beacon Press, 1985).

30. Carolyn G. Heilbrun, *Writing a Woman's Life* (New York: Ballantine Books, 1988), p. 128.

31. Chopp, *Power to Speak*, p. 29.

32. Hardy and Ford, *Praising and Knowing God*, p. 10.

Appendix: Bricolage: Re-formed Praise

1. See Mary Collins, "Feminist Liturgical Principles," *Women at Worship: Interpretations of North American Diversity*, for her insightful "naming" of the principles of ritual practice.

2. See Ronald Grimes, *Ritual Criticism* (Columbia: University of South Carolina Press, 1990), for an account of the ethical issues involved in ritual "borrowing."

3. Nancy Woloch, *Women and the American Experience* (New York: Alfred A. Knopf, 1984), p. 132.

4. Heather Murray Elkins, "Daughter of Jairus," *The New Disciples* (Nashville: EW Press, 1990), p. 16.

5. Heather Murray Elkins, © 1991.

6. Marjorie Procter-Smith, *In Her Own Rite: Constructing Feminist Liturgical Tradition* (Nashville: Abingdon Press, 1990), pp. 36-58.

7. Heather Murray Elkins, "Clean Hands and a Pure Heart: A Liturgy of Basins," *Sacramental Life* (June-August 1989), pp. 16-22.